Education by Design, Not Default

Education by Design, Not Default

How Brave Love Creates Fearless Learning

Janet Newberry

For our grandchildren ~
you are deeply loved.

"Don't only practice your art,
but force your way into its secrets,
for it and knowledge can raise men to the divine."
                                    ~ Ludwig van Beethoven

Contents

Chapter One
Redeeming
Childhood

If this book was the front porch of a small home, nestled among the hills and oak trees in a tiny town, I'd be smiling as you drove up—leaning over the porch rail to welcome you. I've been waiting for you. Can I get you some iced tea? Sweet or unsweet?

I haven't always been the warm and welcoming kind. Most of my life, I tried too hard.

Did your childhood have significant challenges? Mine too. I'm the girl who never fit in the box. In my mind, I didn't belong—even in my own family. Fear lived in our home—invited by "religion," and made a permanent family member because of my mom's mental illness.

My dad was a preacher. I learned at a young age how to dress for church. Shame was my wardrobe consultant. As a preacher's kid, I wore a "Good Enough" mask. I decided showing up as the real me was not a great idea.

If walking on eggshells was an Olympic sport—I would have had a closet full of gold medals. Surviving in a home with mental illness can train people in this odd way of moving through life.

Trusting fear instead of love, my mom's mask of choice was sometimes "Do Not Disturb." As a child, fear planned my daily schedule. Fear. Shame's big brother. Life is a battle for all of us—between fear and love.

I excelled in school, striving in every way to prove there was something worthwhile in me. I woke to a familiar voice each morning reminding me that belonging was still just out of my reach. "Try harder," Shame said, knowing my daily agenda always included more attempts to measure up.

I held the "Don't Rock the Boat" championship title for a long time, too—so it's odd in a fun sort of way that I found freedom from fear while sitting in a lounge chair on the deck of a boat. A big boat. I smile now, remembering it was a "Carnival Cruise"—thinking about all the costumes I had carried on board with me.

Freedom

Freedom came in one sentence—in a book I read four times in five days. "There is nothing you can do to make (God) love you more, and there is nothing you can do to make Him love you less."[1] Really?

I had worked for love my whole life. I pictured Jesus leaning on a mop in the corner of the kitchen every day with a scowl on His face—as I ran in wearing my muddy boots—again.

If you're wondering if you want to keep reading this book because Jesus is in the first chapter, I get it.

---

1 *The Gospel*, J. D. Greer, B & H Depth, 2011

For many years of my life, I would've been tempted to put it down, too.

"Nothing you can do (will) make Him love you more ..." confused me at first. Religion had given me plenty to do—and every day the standards for "good enough" seemed to get higher. For a child with a suicidal parent, shame tells you if you're "good enough" your mom won't kill herself, because she wants to keep being your mom.

I can't write a book about anything "By Design" without writing about God. Fearless freedom is His idea. Some of my favorite people in the world have written a book called, *The Cure*. The subtitle of that book is *What if God isn't who you think He is and neither are you?*

This book, by John Lynch, Bruce McNicol, and Bill Thrall, is written about life and grace. My book is written about life and education ... and grace. Without God we live life by default, not design.

And He's a nice guy. Who knew?

I'm a nice girl, too. Who knew?

When I was 45 years old, I went to the store to buy new dishes. The marriage with my second husband was ending (long story) and I didn't want to fight to keep the stuff I had dragged with me since my first marriage.

I stood staring at all the choices and discovered I didn't know what I liked. Did I like the plates with flowers on them, or the ones with no color but with little raised dots? Did I like white ones or bright ones? It was in the dinnerware department that I realized I didn't know me.

Stunned by my confusion, I lingered in the fog. My choices for the past 45 years had been made by my masks—and my fears. Which choice can I make to be good enough—and loved enough? Which choice can I make so I don't rock the boat? What can I choose to manipulate you to choose what I want?

Slowly and surely, I gave God permission to introduce me to the real me. I listened to Him as He told me who He created me to be. He gave me flowers to enjoy on our morning runs together. And He gave me strength to endure and untangle the life that happens when shame is our tour guide—by default, not design.

Freedom breathed in me when I stopped trying to please God—and a lot of people—trying to fit in the box. With my unveiled face I stopped fighting with life and started playing with it. I stopped fighting with God and started playing with Him, too.

The box I'd kept trying to fit in was bondage—not freedom.

That last sentence makes me laugh. God has a great sense of humor, evidenced by the fact that I'm writing this book while my husband and I are living full-time in an Airstream named Freedom, after selling our house with a slab and four walls. One of the boxes I didn't fit in.

Childhood by design, not default

This book is not going to tell you to sell your house and live in an RV to experience freedom. This book is going to invite you to lighten the load you may be hauling around if fear and shame live in your backpack or briefcase. We can't help our kids if our hands are full of the stuff we're not meant to carry.

The key purpose of this book is to lighten the load our children are carrying—by default, not design.

I read a post on social media just the other day. *"My daughter has played only 30 minutes today. It's 9:00 p.m. and we're still doing homework. She turned 8 a week ago."*

The comments were numerous—and empathetic.

"First and second grade was ok for my kids. Third grade was a beast."

"We haven't made it to bed before midnight for three nights in a row now. Wait until she gets to 7th and 8th grade."

"I want to just let her go to bed, but she has three tests tomorrow—and one the next day. Her grades are not good enough to let her go to bed yet."

This load is too heavy. It's not the childhood our kids are designed to experience and enjoy. But too often it's the childhood our current education system offers them.

If it was bearing good fruit, I might be spending more time defending the system instead of working to change it. But our children are not living full and free lives. They're tired of trying to be good enough. They're burdened with addictions—and carrying the weight of their own immaturity.

There is great hope.

I've had an interesting tour of duty in the service of education. I served twenty years in public schools, seven years in private schools, and five years (and counting) helping homeschool families.

In public school, I was a teacher and an administrator. Thinking I knew what would guarantee success, I stood before my faculty and said, "These children will not fail on my watch." They didn't.

We hung the "Exemplary" sign on the exterior brick walls and cheered. I knew how to get children to perform well on tests. I was the queen of behavior modification. I could make 100 different varieties of sticker charts. During my 20 years in the testing industry, I watched children learn to jump through high hoops.

I watched them pass tests and comply. I didn't often witness children grow up.

A shy young boy in fourth grade passed the test. A few years later he went to middle school diagnosed with anxiety. An angry third grade girl passed the test, too. She went to middle school with the reputation of a bully.

I served as Grammar School Principal in a private school that had a rigorous admission policy. It was clear before a child enrolled: *This school is not a fit for children who struggle.*

But I also served as a teacher and a principal in a private school that didn't use a traditional grading system. The curriculum and philosophy of education was good and true and beautiful. The children enjoyed sitting in real wooden chairs at real wooden desks in rooms with softly painted walls. The children still struggled—with fear and shame.

This private school campus was a model training center. In six years, I met 800 educators from across America and around the world. They came to this little school in the hill country of Texas to learn a new philosophy of education.

All our conversations eventually landed on the same question: What do we do with the children who struggle, who are not good enough to meet the standards? Even adults seem to get lost in the disconnect between struggle and hope.

As a culture, we're losing the battle with struggle. Our children too often hide from it when they can, and find themselves ill-equipped when they can't.

This book is not written to bash public schools—or private schools. This book is not written to advocate for homeschool. This book is written to shed light on assumptions that have been made about education—by default—and offer next steps to take—by design.

The next steps make more sense emotionally, academically, psychologically, and spiritually than our current education system. By design, we learn to appreciate healthy struggle—and grow up. By design, we can stop proving ourselves and fighting to be good—and start playing with life and enjoying what's good.

So, I invite you to linger here, as if this book is a comfortable, safe place to rest and explore. I'll offer a few questions to start our conversation: What if?

What if we're created to grow up in transformational relationships instead of transactional ones—even at school?
What if love is a more powerful fuel than fear?
What if education as we know it is upside down because children are designed to get because they need, instead of getting because they earn?
What if struggle is a gift, by design—not default?

Chapter Two
Transformed,
by Design

When I was a young girl, I loved watching the Olympics. I counted the years between summer and winter games like I counted the days to Christmas. The honed talent of the competitors touched a place deep in my soul. I cheered for Nadia Comaneci as if she were my best friend. I had a front row seat to artistry in motion.

These dreamers had dedicated their time and talents; they had sacrificed their childhood to grow into champions. A professional career awaited many of the chiseled and focused performers when the games were done. They were going to live happily ever after, and they had earned it!

And then I heard the stories of small children in some countries, chosen at very young ages because of a glimpse of talent, who were required to become these amateur stars. It was about compliance, not dreaming. Their country depended on them; their nation wanted to win a medal count. The best coaches in the land would make sure these children would grow up to win. Some of the children enjoyed the training. Most of them feared the consequences if they didn't finish the climb to the top of the medal platform.

This training method is all too similar to our current education system.

Every child in the United States is selected to be a performer; there is no choice but to find their place in the standardized line. Strong ones get to be first; strong ones get to stay first. Schools are counting on their scores. Parents are counting on their grades.

Our country is depending on the performance of our children. Our economy demands we win the competition with other countries. Some children enjoy the training. Many are overcome with the anxiety experienced on the thirteen-year climb from preschool or kindergarten to graduation.

We tell the children that performing well is the road they must travel to live happily ever after. "Get good grades so you can get into a good college so you can get a good job so you can buy a big house and have children and teach them to get good grades..."

I think more children can sing this song than can sing our national anthem.

It is a belief they wrap their lives around, because it is a belief we've wrapped our minds around.

We convince our children they are the god of their future, and if they create enough worth for themselves, they'll create enough life for themselves. We tell them no child will be left behind, but they don't trust us. They see kids left behind all the time. They experience the shame of being left behind, too. Our children don't see too many people living happily ever after... except on a screen.

Tired of transactions

Children don't have an inherent need to perform. We teach them that. **Often, we ask them to perform to meet our emotional needs, not their real needs.** We feel good when our children do well. We think, "They're making good grades ... they're on the winning team ... so we're doing the right thing. Right?" Maybe not.

Our children have a great number of God-given needs, but these needs aren't met by performing. **In a performance-obsessed culture, children experience injuries, instead of maturity.** Their real needs remain unmet while parents and educators (and coaches and tutors) sacrifice to make sure they perform—and win.

We add to the confusion when children do "good"— meaning they win games, make good grades, or get good test scores—and then we allow children to get what they want, because they "earned" it. Children get paid for straight A's. Children are awarded with access to smart phones and computer games, as long as they meet our standards for compliance.

Smart phones don't meet their real needs. The computer games don't either. **But they do numb the pain of their performance injuries, and our culture tells our kids that relating with a screen can be safer than relating with real people.** The virtual world is one of the only places where a whole bunch of people will "like" you, instead of help you, when you do something stupid.

For most kids at first, the virtual world feels like a place where they don't have to be "good" in order to belong—until they realize the virtual world just offers a different standard of "good." It's another performance trap—offering more masks. Our children are stuck in a matrix of toxic vulnerability, chronic immaturity—and addicted to numbing the pain of living life by default.

"Stuck in a transactional childhood" is a helpful description of adolescence. Adolescence is lasting longer and longer in every new generation. Some medical journals report adolescence lasting from the age of 10 until at least age 24. Some reports say it can last until the age of 30.

Childhood, by design, is transformational—not transactional. Our children don't know *what* is wrong with the way they're experiencing childhood—but they do know they've had enough. They feel trapped and ill equipped. A nagging sense of loneliness and insignificance is not settled by earning or deserving.

Transactions may offer grades, prizes, and privileges, but transactions never offer our children a valid identity. Adolescence is a season of identity crisis—resulting from a childhood hijacked by endless earning.

A life of transactions invites our children to wake up every day on a treadmill, watching a performance meter that tells them if they're good or bad. We let the performance meter offer our children their identity. Instead of a low grade simply telling us what still needs to be learned—the grade offers a lie to accompany the low score. "I'm a failure" is the voice our children hear when they struggle to perform.

Earning a 100 on a spelling test doesn't offer helpful truth about identity either. A perfect score on a test is a report of accuracy—nothing more and nothing less. Too often, "I'm good!" is the voice our children hear when they make good grades.

Tests can measure what we know. Grades can reflect our current skill level. But tests never offer what only God can offer—a valid identity, based on relationship, not performance. We learn the truth of who we are from people—not scores.

The earning trap is as tricky with success as it is with failure. Success without love offers a life of immaturity. A life of immaturity has little impact and influence for good in the lives of others—and lacks the real fulfillment we are designed to experience.

Immaturity is adorable when our babies are new. Immaturity is toxic when our children are old enough to have an impact and influence for good in the story of our families—and our world—but they don't. They're missing out on who they were created to be.

Our children know something's missing. They don't sense the satisfaction we've promised will come with perfectionism—and they're exhausted with all the ways their daily schedules require them to "be good." **Too many of our children are surviving on the life-support features attached to the performance treadmill instead of enjoying the freedom of being fully alive.**

Our children's primary need is to experience love, not success. Love will mature them, and can help them be successful—in healthy relationships, not at the expense of them.

Burned out on earning

As adults, we work to earn. We have learned the skills required to earn. We've developed individual passions and talents in mature relationships with others who have taught us the value of our work and of our craft. Adults are designed to earn—and make good use of their earnings.

By design, childhood is a season of learning, not earning. Our children are burned out on earning. Not that long ago, children intrinsically picked up on the manipulative pattern in relationships. Too many of our children get attention and affirmation only when they perform, not because they are our kids.

We are wired to receive attention and affirmation unearned in transformational relationships, not as payment for performing.

We're not designed to work for love. Because our children are not satisfied living in default mode, they've started doing less and demanding more. They don't know they're stuck in a toxic trading game—they just know enough to try to get a better return on their investment. Our kids aren't fooled by the emptiness offered by prizes for performance, and most of them haven't been offered another way of relating.

"Refusing to participate in any more transactions" is a description of entitlement. Entitlement is the toxic fruit of transactional relationships. Relationships are transactional by default, not design.

"I get because I do" is a good idea in business and industry. It works great if I'm buying coffee at Starbucks. *I get* a cup of coffee *because I do* the paying!

"I get because I do" is bondage in relationships.

The weak stay weak in transactional relationships. We are wired for love, not bartering in sacred spaces—like home and family. We forsake our birthright for soup and train our children to stand in the soup line, too.

In transformational relationships, "I get because I need" and "I get because I am loved." And "I get what I need because you're you—and you love me well."

It's not the kind of relationship that gets me a cup of coffee for free, and it is the kind of relationship that gives me what I need to grow up and mature and build the capacity that equips me to struggle well, without shame, so one day I can get more than a cup of coffee!

Relationships that invite children to "Follow me" are the ones that lead them into a big world—where they find significance more than success, at least at first. Think about a young child helping cook dinner or work in the yard. Think about an older child caring for a younger sibling while a parent goes to buy groceries. The young child is not cooking dinner or doing the yard work perfectly. There will be a struggle or two in caring for a younger sibling.

Significance isn't found in our moments of independent perfection. Significance is experienced in a story bigger than ourselves. In the big story of family—where children learn to have impact and influence for good in the lives of others—our children make a valuable discovery. **They discover life—by design.**

When children follow Mom and Dad into a big world, they are invited to experience these truths:

- I am trustworthy.
- I am needed.
- I am growing up.
- I am a dependable helper.
- Others believe in me—and care about my maturity.

- I am learning to live real life in all the ways others invite me to join them and do what I don't yet know how to do on my own—and that I'll need to know to become an adult.

Behavior is the mirror of belief. When children trust the truth that they are dependable, they behave in dependable ways. When they trust that they are needed, children experience the satisfaction that comes when they meet the real needs of a family, a friend, or a classmate.

Our children can experience transformational relationships at school, too. Teachers can offer a rich and rigorous curriculum and invite children to "Follow me. I'll help you if you struggle, but I want you to experience this great book."

School can be a place where children are welcomed to help each other, too. **Children can be trusted and taught how to help, instead of enable.** What a powerful lesson! When school is a safe place to struggle, and a safe place to help each other, children experience a hunger to learn and grow—by design. This is the life we are created to enjoy.

Love is the way.

Love offers transformation, rather than requiring transactions. Our children get what they need to learn and grow up—instead of simply paying all the invoices required of them to graduate.

Moving forward in love is vital; our children must grow. Parents and educators are the road crew. We can build a road of loving transformation. Building this road will be exhausting, by design—not default. Love is always a sacrifice. But the exhaustion of love is deeply satisfying and life-changing.

Growing up in love offers our future more heroes than celebrities. We are created to care for people, not simply perform for them. For those who find themselves on a stage or a field or a screen by design, their performance is for the benefit of others, not just themselves. Talent is a way of loving the world and its people well, not simply using them for personal glory or gain.

The stage, by design, is not a position of power, it is a place of sacred responsibility. And those who stand on it in maturity are ready for this responsibility. They are more than just celebrities, they are people who care.

Children do not live this life in compliance. There is no carrot dangling from a stick to prompt students to take the next step. By design, children travel in trust—and in response to our love. We are heroes, too. Relationships are the pipeline that offer strength to take one step, then another.

Relationships. Not carrots.

Chapter Three
Love, Not Fear

If you're at least as old as I am, you remember having a choice when we stopped at a gas station: leaded or unleaded. In the late 1960's, the massive air pollution experienced in large cities led to increasing emission controls. Car engines changed, too. The new engines required the use of unleaded fuel.

Protecting the environment—and the air we breathe—is vital. Outdoor air is designed to restore and refresh. The formulas we use to make fuel must be safe. Pollution is toxic.

Fear can be toxic, too.

As humans, our bodies are designed to create fuel. Using the nutritional components from the food and beverages we consume, our digestive system finds energy in fats and calories. Our endocrine system produces hormones that regulate growth and development, metabolism, sexual function, reproduction, sleep, and mood—among other things.

Relationships teach our bodies "family recipes" for making fuel. At home and at school, children breathe in a way of formulating energy, using either fear or love as a key ingredient.

Our bodies create clean fuel when we experience relationships that offer us healthy thoughts, habits, and the help we need to struggle well and grow up. As parents and teachers, our children are looking to us to set a precedent for these healthy relationships. They are looking up to discover all that love is designed to provide when our brain releases a chemical called oxytocin.

Oxytocin is the love hormone.

Our bodies create toxic fuel when we experience relationships that offer us fear-based manipulation instead of the help we need to learn, work, struggle, rest, and play. Stimulated by fear, our brain releases a chemical called cortisol.

Cortisol is the fear hormone.

Living in toxic stress, children experience learning problems and anxiety disorders, addictions and depression—and eventually physical illnesses.[2] And when fear is the key ingredient in our daily fuel, maturity stalls—by design.

Cortisol hijacks maturity. Meant for our good, cortisol gives us the energy we need to run away from danger, or to fight for our lives. To give us this kind of "fight or flight" energy, some systems in the body must be shut down. The first systems that turn off are our immune systems, and all forms of new growth.

We're not designed to live in fear. Life happens by default when we experience a daily dose of cortisol. We can survive—for a while—but we don't grow up. And we don't thrive living the life we're designed to

---

2 *The Gift in You*, Dr. Caroline Leaf, Thomas Nelson Publishers, 2009.

enjoy. Education today offers this steady drip of the fear hormone to our children.

Our children don't grow up when they live afraid they won't run fast enough to get the next carrot. Cortisol is the fuel that moves them from struggle to some version of a disorder. They'll get older, and they will carry their struggles with them into their adult lives.

There is always a gap.

This is one thing I've learned in my tour of duty in education. There is always a gap. Every day, children need to move from where they are to a more mature place in their relationships with words and stories, numbers and calculations. Growing up is about closing this gap.

Some children need to grow as readers or listeners; some children need to grow in their habit of attention. All children need to grow. **Growing is natural—and growing is a struggle—by design.**

Closing this gap in love builds maturity. Maturity is the byproduct of experiencing real struggle, protected from fear and shame. This is the design for childhood.

We have done a strange thing with struggle in America's schools. At school, we behave as if struggle is unexpected, a cause for *alarm*, and a sign of a disorder instead of a sign of growth.

We have mapped out a *schedule* for learning subjects and growing up in conduct—as if learning and growing happens at the same speed for everyone. We assume that a good pace and perfect execution of small, uniform steps will prevent any child from struggling.

Well-intentioned, we try to move children from a place of immaturity to a place of maturity without any real struggle.

Our scope and sequence and grade level systems dictate how big of a step each child needs to take in math every day so they don't get "behind." The conduct standards assume every child of the same age has reached a standard level of maturity and they can keep their hands and feet to themselves and listen attentively.

When children can't keep up or follow the rules, they're punished. Punishment looks at a child and says, "Shame on you." As if shame is going to help.

The system assumes all children have legs that are the same length, and they can all take the same size step, and persevere at the same pace, for the same length of time. The pace of instruction assumes all children come to school with the same energy level and hunger for learning.

Because all children don't have legs that are the same length, schools have gotten creative with the ones who are slow to catch on to the regimented performance expectations. Young children are told to move their clip or change their color on a behavior chart.

School policies seem to assume behavior modification systems and rules will surely help children comply. **Children don't get *help* because they need, they get *punished* because they need.**

When students are slow to learn their facts in math, their grades reflect their "delayed development." Children who struggle to sit quietly in class are instructed to sit quietly at recess. Where's the logic in that plan? School procedures seem to assume that punishment is surely the cure and will prevent children from future struggles.

Punishment assumes children need *rehabilitation* when loves says they need *habilitating*. Habilitate is a verb that means to make fit or capable.

Punishment doesn't do that any better than prison does.

For children who are compliantly keeping up, we hand out grades, stickers, extra recess, movies, achievement awards … The air our children breathe at school says learning is performing. It's about keeping up, not about growing up—and impact and influence in the lives of others. It's about "me," and prizes and awards.

There is always a gap. Education needs the hope of closing the gap, starting with the assumption that all children will struggle. Education needs a makeover—so we can connect children to the help they need to confidently expect real transformation.

"A confident expectation" is the definition of hope. Our children need hope.

Helping children grow up

Education is exhausting because it is about helping children grow up. By nature, children are immature and weak. Education is exhausting by nature, not mistake.

Today, teaching is exhausting because it is designed as a system of compliance and performance. Students do what they're told in order to earn what they want or need.

- Students do assignments to earn a grade—and a grade point average.

- Students ask, "Is this going to be on the test?" and study to earn a good test score.
- Teachers give stickers when children return their homework; they give backpack tags when students consistently behave.
- Teachers put marbles in jars when their students do their work quietly.
- Students line up in an orderly fashion so they don't lose the prize of "Fun Friday."
- Students complete community service because it is a requirement for their high school transcript— and they need to show this kind of citizenship on their college applications.
- Teachers give extra credit projects if students need to raise their grade for their report card.

The system today is built on **transactions**. Students are stuck in a "I must do what you say to earn what I need" economy at school. Children live for at least 12 years in this paycheck to paycheck economy. **Every assignment is another bill to pay for what they need.**

A transaction-based childhood runs on toxic fuel.

Students earn good grades on a high school diploma. Some earn a good transcript to earn entrance into a good college. On today's path in education, learning is simply a side effect of living "transaction to transaction" in the school's compliance-based economy.

Cortisol isn't the only problem in the fuel formula we are handing down to our children. Our current education system works because of dopamine.

Did that statement surprise you? Dopamine is meant for our good. It's the hormone that gives us a rush when we get things done. The rush feels good.

Dopamine is created to work in combination with oxytocin. The rush is meant to be a celebration of relationship, and the joy of doing something bigger than myself—with the help of another. We are created to bond with each other. Our hormones are part of this design. **Without oxytocin, dopamine is the hormone of addiction.** At school, this means students get addicted to the prize, instead of to the relationship that is designed to lead them and help them on the journey.

Because bonding is in our DNA, we will bond with something. Without oxytocin, we bond to all the things that are *not designed* to offer peace and, instead become distractions.

Students get addicted to the grades and the stickers; they get addicted to the attention they receive when they perform at a high level. **Or they get addicted to some form of pain relief needed to soothe their over-performance injuries.**

And it's exhausting—for students and educators.

Tomorrow, the teacher must plan another debt to pay. Tomorrow, students wake up to another stack of bills. **Assignments are more like invoices. Children as young as 5 years old can get burdened with a poor credit score.**

We have a word for children who struggle to pay their bills. We call them "behind."

In all my years in education, there's no other word that invites as much fear—in parents or in children—as the word "behind." Fear is shame's big brother. Together, they offer a toxic cocktail as daily fuel.

If love isn't given a chance to wipe out fear and shame—life by default is inevitable.

Adults by Design

No other species on the planet fights against their own maturity. Lacking a desire to grow up is the effect of an auto-immune disease, of sorts. "I don't want to grow up" is an admission that "I don't want to be me." The real me. The real me is designed to be excited about growing up.

When we can market t-shirts for children to wear that say "Don't Grow Up—It's a Trick!" we have swallowed a big lie about being an adult. We believe "adulting" is bad. We believe growing up is something to be avoided, if at all possible.

Lies are more easily believed when we are living life by default. Most of us have been confused for a long time. Something went terribly wrong "in the beginning."

The auto-immune disease started in Genesis, chapter 3, when Adam and Eve decided to trust themselves to build a life based on being good and avoiding evil, instead of trusting God to offer them life—in relationship. All hell broke loose.

Cortisol replaced oxytocin in the family formula for fuel. Maturity got stunted—by fear.

By default, people have tried to be good enough by their own standards ever since—to earn enough money or respect or popularity or toys to distract themselves. Life is unsettling lived by default. We are taught to depend on ourselves more than to trust God and others to help us.

Running on a mix of cortisol and dopamine, life is reduced to a "perform the best you can all by yourself, and then find some pain relief" cycle. We become consumers of all that makes us forget that, no matter how well we perform in a growing number of different categories, we're not finding the satisfaction we are designed to discover.

We're missing delight—by design.

Religion works to convince us we can earn our own righteousness—and that we should. If "should" doesn't work, religion offers fear. Religion offers us life by default—"goodness" based on the law's standards. Not love's standards.

I'm not sure if education followed religion, or religion followed education—but today, both offer life in bondage in a very small box, instead of in the freedom love offers in a very big world. Trying to be good—or right—*to earn* a closer relationship with God is a transactional lie offered to many of us. Believing this lie, we've *worked* too hard for too long *to earn* relationship.

When we believe the lie that performance is the basis of relationship, it's only one more small step to believe the lie that we can work to earn an identity. Whatever identity we earn—a good one, or a not so good one—is the one we live with, by default.

Our good performance is not the basis of relationships. Work is not the way we earn identity, either.

By design, work is one of the ways we discover deep satisfaction, living from the truth of our God-given identity, unless work has been knit together with fear and shame. Work gets knit together with fear and shame when the motive is independent perfection.

Perfection by our own standards is a life according to the law. It is life by default. We have to make the world pretty small to get everything right all by ourselves. Tomorrow we *have to* work; we have to get more. We have to maintain our identity with more earning.

Perfection as a primary motive often encourages selfishness, not relationship. It leaves little room for intimacy. The best I can be is "better than you," based on measurable standards. Helping you costs me something, so I can't afford to give you any of the "goodness" I have worked so hard to earn.

Grace changes everything.

"I have been crucified with Christ. It is no longer I who live, but Christ who lives in me. And the life I now live in the flesh I live by faith in the Son of God, who loved me and gave himself for me," Galatians 2:20, NASB.

Trusting God and His gift of love, we are *given* a new identity—that we could never earn. This gift—of a new heart, and a new nature—is the ultimate transformation.

Disconnected from fear, we discover the truth that we are designed to work and find satisfaction, not shame. Work is satisfying in the ways we are created to build, restore, design, engineer, discover, dream, create, and make the world beautiful.

Working together has more potential for good than working alone. We are wired to live—and work in community. Our children are not created to sit alone in an assembly line model of education, disconnected from meaning and significance. Our children are created to find adventure and delight in a world bigger than they can manage perfectly by themselves.

Have you ever walked into a classroom for young children and seen those 3-sided dividers teachers put up on students' desks so they won't look at each other's work? Too often, *we're afraid* that if children help each other they won't learn. **It's ironic because the only way any of us really learn is when someone helps us.**

We are designed to live in community, noticing real needs and working together—even struggling together—to meet those needs. This is intimacy—and impact. We are created to make the world a better place, in love. We learn to live in the truth of who God says we are. *I'm a lover. You're a lover, too.*

Are you worried about laziness and enabling? Are you thinking that if children are given permission to help each other, some will take advantage of the others—and just copy, instead of really learn?

Maybe. And we can all take advantage of law or love. What if we trust these truths? By design, children want to learn. **By design, children are wired to be hungry for challenge and risk and struggle and, yes, even maturity.**

When there is no prize to be earned by learning, there will be less "stealing" and "cheating" at school. Children steal—by default—to get what they believe they can never earn. Cheating is what happens when fear tells a child to fight for his life.

Learning, by design, is not a way of earning—for a child.

Right answers are something we all want each other to discover and learn ... unless right answers have been reduced to the things we use to earn a prize, and the prize offers me an identity of "better than you."

When love offers to help, children will trust the help that love offers—and really learn. Just like newborn babies, children who trust love will grow up and wrestle with, delight in, and struggle with the fullness of life they were created to enjoy—in relationships. Not alone.

Learning is transformational, not transactional. So is maturity.

"Rest and receive as you abide in Me this day. As your good and faithful Husband,
I lead you by what I supply; not by what I demand, so live freely from My eternal resources.
Live bountifully out of overflow.
For you are not deficient in love, you are sufficient in love.
You are not deficient in gentleness, you are sufficient in gentleness.
You are not deficient in self-control, you are sufficient in self-control.
Nothing by achieving, all by receiving. I am everything you need, simply abide in Me."

~ *Steve Eden*

Chapter Four
What If Struggle
Is A Gift?

"The struggle is real."

Millennials sometimes use the phrase to exaggerate the smallness of their concern. "My favorite nail polish color is no longer available. The struggle is real!" "I had to settle for decaf this morning because we were out of regular. The struggle is real, people."

Struggle has become synonymous with offensive, torturous, to-be-avoided-at-all-costs. Struggle can't be part of the American dream, can it? Other people struggle. Third World countries. Those living in dictatorships with no running water, no food, and fewer than three coffee shops per city block.

We minimize, avoid, or find work-arounds for struggle in the name of convenience and progress. We fight against, pour money into research to fix, and buy gadgets to eliminate struggle. Somehow, the word *struggle* smells of fear.

The truth is, we're afraid of it. Struggle is the "s-word" in our world because it a) sounds like hard work, b) might make us sweat, and c) hints that we're failing at living successfully.

If we struggle in school—where "be good" and "get it right" are the primary goals—we're labeled failures. (A self-label is still a label.)

If struggle is viewed as an enemy of learning, we may have missed the point entirely. If we see struggle as one of life's great negatives, we'll call off marriages, pacify ourselves with activities, and self-medicate our pain. We'll let the fear of struggle push us to distractions that neither solve the struggle or equip us to face it. We'll let toxic relationships fester and hamstring our efforts to grow.

Schools—and families—are conditioned to promote those who learn without struggle and "wonder what to do with" those who do. But what if struggle is a gift, rather than a red flag signaling a failure to perform?

And what if *perform* isn't the real goal?

A story of hope

I once spent a year teaching a young, eleven-year-old girl. I'll call her Mary. At our first introduction, Mary declared her hatred for school. What began early as a struggle in math had grown into full-blown fear.

Despite her mother's ongoing encouragement, Mary refused to read or enjoy literature. Asking her to write anything was like lighting a fuse on a stick of dynamite or pulling the pin on a hand-grenade. Drawing and painting were frustrations for her, too.

Mary despised struggle and feared failure. School was the place where she had lived too long with both.

For the first three or four months of our school year together, Mary and I walked gently into lessons. My priority was developing trust, especially in the ways I offered commitment when she struggled. For many weeks, lengthy games of Uno at a picnic table under a giant shade tree offered an opportunity to hear her story. She began to breathe more deeply. Dragging her pain into the light seemed to lessen its grip on her heart. Being outdoors was a healing place for Mary. Relationship was too.

Together we wrote numbers on dry erase boards—endlessly and every day. Counting by odds and evens, forward and backward ... Numbers began to delight Mary instead of destroy her.

Discovering patterns and predictability seemed to invite Mary to trust math, instead of hate it. She developed enough strength to do one page of work, then two. Because it was safe to ask for help, Mary most often forgot her fear of failure.

When her grandmother came to visit her at school before our Christmas break, Mary declared with confidence, "Math is my favorite subject." Before the summer break, Mary had covered two and a half years of math curriculum in just nine short months.

Together Mary and I lingered tenderly in Scripture and stories. Her heart had a fondness for the Bible. She already knew it well. Conversations flowed freely—about fear and faith. In Hannah Hurnard's *Hinds Feet on High Places,* Mary took the journey to the High Places with Much Afraid. It was a healing climb. Words poured out of her unlocked heart—on paper, too. By Christmas, Mary was a self-proclaimed writer!

Struggling well in truth

January brought a new subject to go along with the new year. Mary was writing more words than her young hands could handle. She wanted to learn to type on a computer, so "Keyboarding" joined the other subjects listed in the daily schedule. We downloaded the Mavis Beacon typing tutorial program, and Mary sat up straight—with high hopes. Her fingers found their place on the home keys. The first exercise began.

But within seconds, Mary's hands ran away from home, following the fear that now darkened her mood. Her arms crossed tight against her struggling heart. She had hit the wrong key. Mary had made a mistake. The computer had announced her mistake with a corrective buzzer, and the buzzer seemed to pronounce her struggle too strongly for her prideful preference.

"I can't do this!" she snorted. "I'll never learn how."

I watched her disappear. She ran away from her hopes; she ran away from her heart. Mary pulled out her old mask, like a familiar sweatshirt that had kept away the cold. Any comfort from me was pushed away with shame.

"I'm stupid," she shouted. "You hate me."

Behavior is the echo of belief.

This disappearing act lasted for days. It might have lasted longer, if I had not started transcribing her outbursts on the dry-erase board that hung on our dining room wall. I wrote down all her words; they made a long list. When she was able to find a mustard seed of faith, we looked at the list together. We agreed to label the list "Lies."

And we made another list.

Next to all the lies we wrote the truth. Beside "I can't do this!" we wrote "I can do this." Next to "I'll never learn how!" we wrote "I can learn how."

And we erased the word "Keyboarding" in the list of subjects scheduled for the day. We gave the subject a new name: "Struggling well in truth" now came right after Math, and right before lunch.

Mary's instructions for what used to be "Keyboarding" were simple. Her goal was not building speed or improving in accuracy. Whenever the buzzer announced she'd made a mistake, Mary was to look at the board and declare the truth.

Buzz! "I can do this." *Buzz!* "I can learn how."

Buzz! Truth. *Buzz!* Truth.

The pattern repeated for days; then weeks. By the time we hugged each other and said, "Have a great Spring Break!" Mary was typing 35 words per minute with 98% accuracy. Mary had trusted love to untangle the lies; the truth had taught her to type.

Mary's mom and I are still friends, now four years later in Mary's story. I sent my friend an email to ask permission to use this retelling. My heart laughed out loud when I received this fun news as part of her mom's reply.

"She has been writing a novel now for the past several months. She's at around 89,000 words and spends probably 10-15 hours a week working on it!"

Love equips, not enables. This is our great hope.

What stories are we telling ourselves?

All struggle is not bad struggle. Trauma is bad struggle; children need our protection from trauma. Growing requires good struggle. Growing comes with growing pains. **Do our children know the difference between the pain of trauma and the pain of good struggle that produces maturity and strength?**

What stories do our children tell themselves when they struggle? Or when we struggle? Or when their peers struggle? What stories do *we* tell ourselves when we struggle? And when our children struggle? If the stories we believe are not true, we experience life in a kind of matrix. The reality we have built for ourselves is not real. When we trust lies, we do not experience the freedom of truth.

For almost eleven years, Mary had been afraid of struggle and failure. What emotion have *we* attached to struggle? And to experiences that are hard? If we live in a performance-obsessed culture with expectations of perfection, we may "hate" struggle. We may loathe "hard."

What if it's not true? What if when our children struggle, they could make these trades?

- Not "I hate school" but "I hate the way I've always experienced school."
- Not "I hate reading" but "I hate what I've experienced about reading with immature books and prizes or grades for answering questions or writing book reports."
- Not "I'm stupid" but "I need help and no one has ever told me that needing help is normal."
- Not "I'm ADHD" but "I need help developing my habit of attention."

In our pursuit of a struggle-free life, or a day that's not hard, what do we get to experience? A full and free life doesn't happen with bumper pads. How do our children learn that there's really no such thing as a "no sad" day? Or a "no hard" day? Or a day when all of their expectations are met in their fullest measure?

As parents, are we making our children's world too small so they can get it all right? Or so they don't have to struggle?

How do our children learn to trust the experience of joy that comes at the same time as the pain of good struggle?

Struggle, by Design

Life by default requires me to earn an identity—by performing, and being "good enough." I'm performing to earn prizes, too—needed to distract me from the nagging feeling that "something's just not right."

"Why am I not satisfied?"

There is no good place for struggle in a life lived by default. Struggling to perform means I'm struggling to *earn*. Cortisol increases—and it backfires in all the ways my brain shuts down when I'm afraid.

Life by design—on the other hand—offers me a new, sacred identity. God knew we'd struggle. He knew we'd need help. Thank you, Jesus—a new shame-free identity is ours for the trusting.

Restored to new life, my new identity comes with a new routine. Each day I am designed to trust and experience satisfaction in real work, good struggle, leisure, play, and rest. **Struggle is not a reason to be afraid.**

By design, struggle is part of real life.

Struggle invites us to connect with people we trust who can lend us strength. Relationships help by protecting us from fear—and reminding us of the truth, in place of the lies.

Struggle invites us to work hard, and experience real fulfillment because we persevered through struggle—not because we avoided it. When safe relationships protect me from shame, I experience the love that helps me mature.

Struggle is an invitation to humble myself and grow up. This is living!

Chapter Five
Education by Default

Imagine the first day of school in September, 1951. As a child, you would have arrived unaware that you were making history—part of an unprecedented crowd of over four million students nationwide. As a teacher, you would have watched five times more students than you expected walk through the doors of your school. The firstborn children of the Baby Boom entered classrooms five years later like a tidal wave following a distant earthquake.

"In an hour's time on that first day of school, (over 4.2 million) children forced a total change in the system. Almost overnight educators threw together what was later described as 'a maladaptive response to a crisis situation' and called it public education."[3]

In the initial chaos, the loudest voices got the most attention, and assumption and efficiency spoke louder than wisdom. Assumption said that all ten-year-olds would be ready for the same thing on the same day.

---

3 Raising Self-Reliant Children in a Self-Indulgent World, H. Stephen Glenn & Jane Nelsen, Ed.D., Prima Publishing, 1987

Wisdom tried to remind those rushing to establish skill-level reading groups that individual differences were things of value and reasons for appreciation. "Differences offer more to a group than they require," she said.

Wisdom was ignored in favor of efficiency. Fear spoke up, too. Many teachers were afraid of losing control.

Instead of being invited into multi-age learning communities, and at the expense of meaningful dialogue and collaboration, children were sorted by age into grade-levels. Mass-production soon described both curriculum and cafeteria food. During the next several decades, schools began to look more like factories than safe places to learn. Education became an industry. **Schools became the places children went to work more than to grow up and learn.**

Performance-obsessed cultures became the norm. Education by default planted the seeds that have grown into significant false traditions. Students became products to be measured. Educators seemed to forget they were supposed to relate with children *in loco parentis* (in the place of a parent,[4]) and children became test scores to be ranked and marketed, instead of persons to be raised, nourished, known, and valued.

Children growing up in America after the end of World War II experienced a whole new world. As fresh hope welcomed home the surviving heroes and prosperity entertained a new phenomenon of two-income families, the children born into this new culture unknowingly faced life without many of the traditions that had served their ancestors well.

---

4   https://www.merriam-webster.com/dictionary/

Children of the 50s and 60s were no longer raised in the lifestyles of their parents and grandparents which had provided much in the way of opportunities for growing up. Traditions that once provided hours of apprenticeship and on-the-job training for real life skills were lost to new ways of relating—with same-aged peer groups, television, and developing technology.

Traditions are life-giving when they offer rituals rooted in truth and ways of relating that build strength. Many of the traditions offered to the generations born after World War II have been rooted in response to emergencies—not truth. Many of the new ways of relating have left children vulnerable, instead of protected and growing stronger.

False traditions are rituals and norms of society that are formed when wisdom is ignored in favor of efficiency, unsettled emotions, or control. When false traditions build the roads on which our children travel, many of the stories they tell themselves are not true. Our children are struggling—tripped up by false traditions, and void of mature strength. This is education by default.

America's children are struggling.

Childhood, by design, is a season of promise and hope. A full and free life opens before our youngest ones like the fresh pages of a new book. Those of us who are no longer the youngest write our children's stories with a "happily ever after" ending.

But they're not. Our children are not living happily ever after. They're bearing their own issues, taking on the burdens of their friends, families, and the world at large, and are carrying their struggles into their adult lives.

Anxiety colors their world so completely that it wouldn't be surprising to see a new shade in the Crayola box.

The statistics are staggering:

- "More than 1 in 20 US children and teens have anxiety or depression."[5]
- More than 6 million children struggle with ADHD.[6]
- School shootings have become a trend.
- On average, from 1999-2015, one child under the age of 13 died of suicide every five days.[7]
- "More than 30 million (grow into) adults in the United States (who) cannot read, write, or do basic math above a third grade level." —*ProLiteracy*[8]

There is a vast gap between the lives we dream of for our children and the lives they are living. The gap is growing, like a widening chasm when tectonic plates shift. The path moving us from real struggle to real hope seems hard to find.

Not a safe place to learn

I don't remember much of what I learned in college, but I do remember this: One professor said, "Confusion precedes real learning. If you're not confused, you already know."

---

5   https://www.sciencedaily.com/releases/2018/04/180424184119.htm
6   http://www.chadd.org/understanding-adhd/about-adhd/data-and-statistics/general-prevalence.aspx
7   *https://www.cnn.com/2017/08/14/health/child-suicides/index.html*
8   https://education.cu-portland.edu/blog/education-news-roundup/illiteracy-in-america/

Education today is not kind to confusion. Confusion is to be avoided. Confusion invites fear, and shame, and hiding. Confusion attracts bullies. Confusion often ends up with a label.

When education is not kind to confusion, school is not a safe place to learn.

Confusion is a kind of struggle. When we are not left alone in our confusion, persevering produces maturity.

"Not alone" in school today is often called "cheating." "Independent practice" is the last step in every lesson cycle. Every lesson includes a test. Children are left alone—even *required* to be alone—in their academic struggle at school.

At school, we expect children to independently master skills. If children struggle, we require a documented "qualifying condition" before teachers are allowed to consistently help them.

Needing help or struggling at school are experiences "regular" children don't have. Struggle is connected to fear—not love. Not maturity.

Alone, without consistent help, and afraid to struggle, children travel a road in school that is full of potholes and dangerous curves. **Navigating the road longer or at a slower pace doesn't untangle struggle. It prolongs problems.**

It inflames struggle and invites our children to hide. They hide behind screens and bad moods. **They hide in the ditch of adolescence ... and sometimes never emerge.**

What is meant for our good—struggle that leads to growth—is toxic at school. Because struggle is "not

41

good," relationships become fear-based in all the ways our children keep trying to measure up and get it right.

Distraction doesn't resolve their struggles. Shame disconnects our children from hope.

Aiming at the wrong target

Too many schools are living the tragedy of Matt Emmons in the shooting competitions of the 2004 Olympics. As reported in USA Today, with one bullet left to shoot, all Matt Emmons needed was a score of 7.2 to win his second gold medal of the Olympic Games. On his first nine shots in the finals, Emmons' lowest score was a 9.3. He took careful aim, fired … bull's eye.

But Emmons' shot pierced the wrong target—known as a crossfire—resulting in a score of 0. Instead of gold, Emmons, 23, of Browns Hill, N.J., was left trying to explain the rare mistake that left him in eighth place.

Emmons' last shot hit a perfect bull's eye in lane two. He was competing in lane three.

As educators we are cross-firing, too.

At some schools, after spending a great deal of money, time, and effort on new programs, we are hitting a perfect bull's eye—on the performance target. The adults hang the "exemplary" commendation on the brick exterior, too often not noticing the injuries this great weight has inflicted on the lives of the young burden bearers.

What if the performance target is in lane two, but we are created to live in lane three?

Traditional education aims at the target of performance. Children are required to perform daily. School is a job—even for a five-year-old.

The fuel that powers children on this path is fear. Fear hurts and fear hates. Many students hate reading or hate math. Some students hate each other. "Performance obsessed cultures can never promote healing. They only create more wounding."[9]

I'll offer this two-sentence summary of my research:

When we aim at the target of performance, maturity always suffers.

When we aim at the target of maturity, performance goes off the charts.

What is maturity?

Maturity is like the wind. We can't see it, but we can clearly see evidence of it. We can feel and experience maturity's impact and influence or the lack of it. Maturity isn't evidenced by age, natural talent, or the ability to please or perform with perfect execution, although skill level increases as a result of maturity.

Maturity is transformation. It is the resolution of immaturity that love offers, by design.

We experience the supernatural miracle of maturity when we let someone meet our real needs unconditionally. We don't earn; we receive.

We see this kind of safe relationship clearly between parents and infants. It's literally impossible for a newborn to *earn* a diaper change or a feeding. An infant experiences maturity when the little one trusts and freely receives the love that meets their needs.

We don't often call an infant "immature." Immature is a word we use to describe someone experiencing less than they were created to discover and enjoy during

---

9   trueface.org

their designated stage of development. When an infant's needs are met, they discover a big world and enjoy growing up.

We sometimes describe an infant as "fussy." A fussy infant is a little one who is still building trust, and who needs someone to help them discover that joy is designed to be our normal state.

Joy means "it's good to be me, here with you." In struggle and in delight—it's good to be me here with you. It's good because we're together. We trust each other—for help and protection. We're designed to be loved, and to love one another.

 Returning to joy from every unpleasant emotion is the hallmark of emotional fluency. The ability to return to joy indicates a mature (or maturing) emotional immune system. It is the signature of mental health. Returning to joy means I trusted another and experienced their love.

Love is joy's big brother. Love protects me from lies—and from staying stuck in a painful or angry place. Love helps and love heals. It's good to be me here with you because of love. Love is the fuel of maturity.

By design, maturity builds capacity. Childhood follows infancy. Parents and caregivers provide the unconditional love that meets the God-given needs of children, and the love that says "no" to the immature wants that don't meet real needs. Wants are immature when they don't help children grow up.

Love protects from bondage. Parents are designed to protect children from addictions.

Many of a child's real needs are met when loving parents and adults invite a child to "Follow me" into

44

the real world. Childhood is meant to prepare children for adulthood, so it is the season of life designed to be spent learning to "take care of myself."

In an honest childhood, children learn how to live in all the ways of getting dressed, cleaning up their room, working around the house, washing dishes, mowing the yard, solving math problems, reading, writing, ... and returning to joy from every unpleasant emotion.

Real needs and real struggles are invitations to connect in helpful relationships—and learn. Because children trust—and get help—they grow up.

Childhood has become a confusing season for parents, so it has become a confusing season for children. By default, parents forget that children don't *need* to perform. They *need* to learn.

Our performance-obsessed culture is killing childhood. I'm surprised we haven't started labeling our children with a mowing disorder, or a dishwasher disorder. When children experience struggle—we get triggered by shame. We panic. We helicopter. We justify. We blame.

Children don't mow the yard because they're good at it. They mow the yard because they need to learn how to do it well—and they need someone to help them learn. Children don't clean the bathroom because they're naturally good at it. They clean the bathroom because they need to learn how to do it well—and they need someone to help them learn.

Childhood has become a confusing season for educators, too. An honest childhood is a season when children learn to read—not when they're expected to read without help. Childhood, by design, is a season when children learn to spell and do math without being labeled because they need help.

Making life easier so children can do things by themselves isn't the purpose of childhood. Life isn't easy, by design.

Children simply need us to help. Our children need us to say, "Follow me" and they need us to understand that they're learning—not performing. Too often, we become afraid when our children need help. Shame enters the story—invited by fear.

Fear and shame attract lies.

Maturity happens in truth, not lies.

Maturity is evidenced when "I know who I am" and "I know who I'm not"—truthfully. Immaturity is evidenced when I believe a lie about who I am. "I'm stupid" and "I'll never be good at this" are spoken in immaturity.

Maturity is evidenced when "I know who you are" and "I know who you're not"—truthfully. Immaturity is evidenced when I believe a lie about who you are. "You're stupid" and "Loser!" are spoken in immaturity.

Vulnerability is natural in infancy and childhood. Parents and adults (teachers) are created to provide the protection children need to grow up—into maturity. This is love.

Vulnerability waves a red flag—"At Risk"—after the age of twelve. Children who don't grow up equipped to be young adults, and who can't ask for help when they need it, will spend years stuck in the ditch of adolescence.

Some adolescents never experience life as a mature adult, and instead become immature parents—not equipped to protect their children. Without communities of grace, the maturity of entire families is now at stake. **Ultimately, prolonged immaturity is devastating to the culture of a nation.**

Immature people are at high risk of believing lies, falling prey to the schemes of those willing to take advantage of the weak for their own gain, and handing down family addictions. Immature parents are not equipped to offer the next generation freedom—and real hope.

Immaturity limits our capacity to enjoy life—until more mature people reach out and build relationships that offer to help. Trust is built with honesty. Immaturity ends with humility.

Maturity is evidenced by honesty and humility. Maturity is evidenced when I see myself and my skills and abilities truthfully—and ask for help when I struggle.

These are mature statements from a child:

"Running fast comes naturally for me."

"Will you help me with my math?"

"I need help learning to cook healthy meals."

Maturity is evidenced when I see others and their skills and abilities truthfully, too.

These are mature statements from a parent—or teacher:

"I know reading is a struggle for you right now, and you're trusting good help. You're learning."

"How can I help you with your homework?"

"You have a natural ability for baseball."

Maturity is evidenced by relationships of trust. A relationship of trust is like a vine and a branch. The branch stays connected to the vine, by design. The vine feeds it and makes it possible for the branch to bear good fruit. The branch needs the vine—and the branch is created to offer something good to the world.

We are designed to find deep satisfaction as a contributor, not simply a consumer. Growing up is about helping others—and meeting their real needs as they travel their own road to maturity. The ability to care for at least one other person—while maintaining personal integrity—is a key indicator of a mature young adult.

Adolescence is life by default.

Adolescence is characterized by immaturity. It's the fruit of a childhood lived in the lies of default. "It's all about me" is only adorable in infancy. Selfishness is depressing as a teenager. "I can't help" or "I don't have to help" are the words of an immature person experiencing an identity crisis. Entitlement is adolescence on steroids.

Adolescents are not to blame for adolescence. They are responsible for being a part of the resolution of the struggle, but they are not responsible for creating this default season of life—that is not part of our original design.

Prior to the 20th century, there is no record of the word "adolescence." Puberty and adolescence are not synonyms. Puberty is a physical stage of development—designed to be experienced with the maturity of a young adult, not an adolescent.

Adolescence metastasized during a season in American history when families weren't prepared to raise one of the first generations ever to experience childhood with both parents working outside of the home. Without parents that said, "Follow me,"—into the kitchen and into the yard, into the office and onto the farm—children didn't learn many of the basic skills required to become an adult.

When children don't learn, they experience a nagging sense of being ill-equipped, and they don't grow up to be young adults. They get stuck. They don't know why they feel ashamed—and they also feel afraid. When children are slow to learn and grow up, parents deal with fear and shame, too.

Adolescence is a delay in natural development. Stagnation attracts lies. Historically, we began to believe the lies—about ourselves, about our children, about childhood, and about struggle. We forgot that childhood is a season of natural struggle—because it is a season of learning and growing.

And we keep forgetting the truth. Without our own relationships of trust, we'll choose a solution to the struggle offered by fear or shame. We'll blame, shame, justify, enable, deny, label, or punish—instead of love.

Struggling with prolonged immaturity, we're now handing children "good enough" masks in a myriad of different performance arenas. Immaturity is never good. Immaturity is a synonym for vulnerable. We need the protection of love.

The evidence of maturity is our capacity to be loved and to love others. We experience the power and practicality of love because we're created with real needs—and because struggle is a part of growing up. Others experience our love, too.

At school, a mature reader is not simply someone who can make an exemplary grade on a standardized test. A mature reader is someone who has good skills in reading and a deep affection for great books, and who shares their affection and skill with others so they can become mature readers, too.

At school, a mature student is not simply someone who stays out of trouble and earns good grades. A mature student is someone who leads others away from trouble and helps them when they struggle.

Children spend their childhood in school. If education continues to aim at the target of performance, the very fabric of our families—and our nation—will continue to unravel.

When we remember that children learn and grow because we live life with them, help them struggle well in truth, and protect them from lies—and anything that might hijack their maturity—we offer our children an honest childhood.

When we offer our children an honest childhood, we offer the world trustworthy adults. We'll need to help each other change the aim of education.

Education, by design, aims at maturity.

Chapter Six
Imagine
Education
Transformed

Schools are supposed to help children learn and grow up. By design, education is given as a gift, and received in trust—and humble submission. Maturity happens naturally. Learning does too. Can you imagine?

A gift, not a transaction.

Given, not earned.

Received in trust, not required in compliance.

When education is transformational, everything changes. Because there is no fear in love—asking for help is safe.

"Follow me," says the teacher.

"I trust you," says the student.

And the real adventure begins—by design.

Humility, not shame

I remember vividly the day I experienced Sir Peter Paul Ruben's enormous painting of *Daniel in the Lion's Den* in the National Gallery of Art. The size of the canvas, the colors, the shadows, the lions, and the trusting and desperate Daniel—the encounter was an invitation to linger, rather than to rush. A thoughtful artist had set his canvas on an easel nearby. He was lingering, too. Sir Ruben was his art instructor; the giant painting was his lesson.

Reproductions are the way young artists grow in their craft. They copy the work of more advanced artists. Sitting at the feet of a master offers a literal big picture look at detail and technique, layered with great care—and the kind of wisdom that comes with years of experience. We are all maturing artists. Perhaps we've never been told.

What we see, we do. What we hear, we repeat. We learn to speak with many words, or with a few. Our personal vocabulary account is a gift acquired in our relationships.

Life exists for us in a full and free world, or a small and trivial one. We have followed others who lead us, either into a tiny place that requires us to please, or into a big world that reminds us to humble ourselves in a safe place—and trust.

We copy those we trust—for better or worse. We ignore or engage. We judge or affirm. We linger in leisure or have a voracious appetite for entertainment.

If those we trust are wise and generous in their care, we will grow up by following their lead. If those we trust meet our real needs, we'll grow strong because we trust their direction and correction. If those we trust don't meet our real needs, we will grow older—but not more satisfied.

By design, education offers an atmosphere and curriculum that reminds children daily of their true identity and their sacred place in relationship. He is a child of God; she is a child of God. A child's place in relationship is the place of trusting and receiving. Learning happens in humility, not humiliation.

As children grow up, they learn to offer themselves to the world in worthy conversations and good work. They have something to say because they are abiding in real books and lingering in thought-worthy ideas. Children learn to speak the language of the wise. They learn to paint. They learn to draw. They learn to build and create.

Learning happens in a trusting posture of submission.

"*Submission* is a love word, not a control word. Submission means letting someone love you, teach you, or influence you. In fact, the degree to which we submit to others is the degree to which we will experience their love, regardless of how much love they have for us. Submission goes hand in hand with vulnerability."[10]

Vulnerability is vital as a learner. The weak become strong because they are loved well—not because they are labeled, or afraid.

Imagine a world where children wake up inspired to go to school, feel connected in safe relationships, and go to bed fulfilled at the end of the day. This is education by design, not default.

Inspired to go to school

By default, a classroom in a traditional school is crowded with laminated posters, bright plastic pencil boxes, sticker charts, marble jars, and treasure trunks. A child's

---

10 *The Ascent of a Leader,* Bill Thrall, Bruce McNicol, & Ken McElrath, Jossey-Bass, 1999.

eyes are drawn in endless directions; sensation is everywhere. Reminders are everywhere, too—of transactions that must be paid to maintain a satisfactory status in the classroom community.

A child knows he or she must please the teacher so they don't have to change their color or move their clip on the *behavior modification board*.

They must complete all their work independently if they're going to join their classmates at recess.

Sticker charts are accounts payable ledgers. Completing assigned reading, turning in homework, and memorizing math facts are all done so one student's row of stickers is as respectable as another's.

By default, classrooms are transactional—saturated with endless ways each child must continually *earn* their status and *maintain* it.

By design, inspiration is everywhere at school—not sensation. Children receive attention, direction, correction, significance, acceptance, security, and affirmation—because they need this love to grow up, and to do the real work of school and life. The weak become strong because they are well nourished—with good books, rich language, attentive relationships, and an atmosphere of care rather than manipulation.

Transformation is the way we are created to live and grow. We may be fooled by the pattern of industry. We may demand that even young children receive because they earn, but human beings are designed to become what they receive.

When children trust and receive love, *they become* lovers—of all that love has offered. They will love one another, too, because they have been offered relationship. When children trust and receive trinkets and prizes and marbles in jars, *they become* addicted to these sensational rewards—and live in bondage to the many ways they must continually work to pay for more of them.

Inspiration offers children something internal first—strength and support and influence. Having received, children are equipped to work and create and solve and build.

In contrast, sensation holds out an external prize, like a treat for a dog. Left to perform using their own immature strength, children check boxes, fill in blanks, and color in tiny circles on testing sheets—striving to please, so they can earn.

Sensationalism becomes an addiction; the weak stay weak. John Lynch's words (used by permission) describe the dilemma of education by default: "I wonder if many of us medicate ourselves with pursuits that don't give life because we haven't yet learned how to enjoy ourselves in the moments that offer life."

Education by design offers children this transformational life.

Connected in safe relationships

We are created for connection. By design, we need relationships with God and others. Without healthy connections, the weak can't become strong. Absent of relationships that love us well, we experience rejection, low self-esteem, and a loss of hope. Without protective love—and the love that offers us direction and correction, we experience a misguided life, a loss of identity, and a lack of security.

Even if we can provide for our basic needs of food, clothing, and shelter, without trusting relationships, our lives lack meaning and purpose. We may survive, but we won't thrive.

When our imperfection combines with our fear of being ignored or rejected, fear becomes our mode of operation. Love happens in our moment of need, not perfection. When we have to be perfect in order to be affirmed or accepted or paid attention to, we miss the "unforced rhythms of grace," Matthew 11:28-30, MSG.

The chemicals in our bodies are designed to help us experience the fullness of life—but only in caring relationships. Oxytocin combines with other chemicals—such as dopamine and serotonin—to help us get things done and achieve our goals.

Without oxytocin, serotonin tricks us to acquire status symbols (designer clothing, expensive purses, fast cars...) as a way of feeling like a leader, without any honest benefit to others, or the deep satisfaction of real impact for good in our community. **What is meant for our good is a recipe for disaster, without the protective power of love.**

Education by design knows the benefits of love. Children don't love Literature and Mathematics and History and Science because these subjects require them to prove they are proficient. We don't fall in love in relationships that demand us to perform.

Education by design offers life less alone, blessed by varied and deep relationships with a wide range of subjects, writers, and books—offered to children by teachers who are trusted guides, leading them into new discoveries. When children experience the love *given to them* by Nature and Music and Art, they find love growing in their own hearts for these subjects, too.

When History offers children direction and significance, the natural response is a love of History. When Science offers security and protection, the natural response is a love of Science. God is in Nature, Literature, and Math—and children can find something of His love there. Children are transformed by what is offered. They trust—and grow up in mutually satisfying relationships.

We have all seen this "we love because He first loved us" miracle happen when a little boy receives the gift of a new puppy. The puppy showers the young one with endless licks with his scratchy tongue, and he joyfully high-fives his master with a million wags of his tail. The little boy is in love!

We've seen it happen with a young girl and a runt pig. In the children's classic, *Charlotte's Web*, Wilbur thrived because of Fern's commitment and servant love, offered in response to his gift of loving trust.

"Love always trusts," I Corinthians 13:7, NIV.

And Fern with a runt pig, like a young boy with a new puppy, needs a mature parent to help navigate the new relationship. "Mrs. Arable found a baby's nursing bottle and a rubber nipple. She poured warm milk into the bottle, fitted the nipple over the top, and handed it to Fern. 'Give him his breakfast,' she said."[11]

Fern's mom helped her navigate the new relationship of trust.

Children need help navigating relationships of trust with school subjects, too. Draw a triangle, in the margin

---

11 *Charlotte's Web*, E. B. White, Harper & Row, 1952.

of this page, if you will—or draw one simply in your mind. Make it the kind that has a flat bottom and a point on the top.

By default, the student sits at one end of the bottom line and a school subject sits at the other. The teacher sits at the top—requiring the student to make independent transactions with each subject.

By design, the subject sits at the top of the triangle. The teacher sits near one end of the bottom line, and the student sits near the other. The teacher and the student sit side by side, together experiencing the transformation the subject offers. The teacher lends strength, and the student grows stronger.

This is the picture of transformational relationships in education. Struggles come untangled before they last too long and become fearful knots. Brave love protects the child's identity from shame. Because school is a safe place to struggle, it's a safe place to learn.

Fulfilled at the end of the day

It was the last day before the Christmas break—normally "Christmas party day" at school. It was my first year teaching at a small, private school in the Texas hill country. Students and teachers at this school based on the Charlotte Mason philosophy enjoy a different tradition each year on this day. I was as curious as one of the new students assigned to my group.

Instead of a party, the students were organized into Christmas caroling groups and sent with teachers and chaperones into the shops on Main Street and the far corners of this small town. The children—well coached in offering themselves in song—poured out the blessings of the season on tourists and tired business owners, in taverns and on tiny porches.

Some groups visited the hospital; some the Assisted Living centers. This particular year, it didn't take long before the joy the children were sharing began to spill over in greater measure into their own hearts.

"It is more blessed to give, than receive," Acts 20:35, NIV.

After the third stop on our groups' caroling route, the new student—I'll call her Clara—exploded as we were piling back in the car to move to our next assigned destination.

"I get it! Now I understand what we're doing! Can we please go sing to my uncle? He needs this kind of cheer. Can we please?"

She went on to tell everyone in the car about his addictions and financial setbacks—as she was begging me to add her uncle's house to our caroling route.

Clara lived in the foster care of her aunt and uncle. It was a recent transformation for all of them. Struggle wrapped around the circumstances in her life like wild morning glory vines on an oak tree. This Christmas caroling morning, she was showing all her glory!

Clara's uncle smiled through tears of joy as his heart seemed to rest in the notes of Christmas songs offered shamelessly from full-hearted children. Her aunt insisted each of us take handfuls of homegrown persimmons—offered like gold, frankincense, and myrrh to the people who delivered baby Jesus right to their front yard.

We finished our route and returned to campus to enjoy Christmas cookies and hot chocolate before hugs and shouts of "Merry Christmas!" scattered the children to their homes for the holidays. Clara proudly shared her delight with anyone who would listen to the Christmas story that she had experienced this day.

Purposeful, not perfect. Belonging, not estranged. True, not convenient. Known, not labeled.

Shame had no attachment to Clara's story—not on this sacred day, at least. She shared her freedom like the Samaritan woman who ran back to town after she met Jesus at the well. Her uncle's tears had washed the feet of those of us who'd brought good news.

Disconnecting struggle from truth never offers relief from shame. Only when we are fully alive and authentic in our struggles can we be intimately comforted by the gifts of love. We can teach our children to offer these gifts, too—and watch them run to share them with others.

Chapter Seven
Where Do We Begin with Young Children?

The children in the small classroom were four and five and six years old. Their enthusiasm for life was fresh—as was their eagerness this day in Picture Study. The teacher wisely instructed the young ones to carefully handle the picture reproductions she was about to hand out, and she also told them there were more children than there were pictures to distribute.

"You will need to share," she said, which was followed by a collective groan.

The groan received no correction or consequence. It came and went—resolving itself without any fixing from the teacher. She was leading the children in peace, rather than correcting or medicating their age-appropriate reaction.

Her subconscious thought was, "Maturity will come."

As she handed out the pictures to the children—each anticipating the hand-off more than a poor man wishing for a winning lottery ticket—a little boy huffed at being passed over and required to "Look on with your friend."

The wise teacher skipped the speech about "Life's not fair" and didn't choose the "I'm so sorry—you'll get to be first next time" oration, either. Instead she reached out and gently tousled the young boy's hair.

"You're loved," she said.

And it was settled. His spirit. He was reminded, not reprimanded. Healing hands and words of commitment kept the young lad's heart open—and his mind stayed open, too. Maturity had visited this moment with him. Stringing enough of these moments together, love will one day turn this little boy into a man.

What other moments and memories can we string together for young children? What convictions can we offer that may spare them from natural consequences?

Let's begin at the beginning—by design, not default.

Keep relationships first.

Education by design offers opportunities to live a new life that prioritizes connection, rather than control or achievement. **Don't make the world so small that your child can get everything right by themselves.** Instead of spending too much time alone on immature workbooks or computer-based activities, children need more mature lessons.

Homeschool moms, on days when you're tired, or running low on capacity, consider this: It's better to schedule less time for school that day than to teach your child that school is about completing immature work independently. Seize the opportunity to develop a hunger for school, and a love for real life—nothing less.

Begin mature routines.

Routines offer the rhythm of either a mature life, or an immature one. The difference lies simply in the routines we allow to become personal habits. Help your child establish a morning routine that is a mutually satisfying experience in your home. The habit of grumpiness or excessive prompting is just that—a habit. The habit of cheerfulness, and care about the impact and influence one has on the family can become a habit, too.

If your child wakes up slowly, teach them to set an alarm so they have more time to move slowly at first and still be their "best self" when it's time to engage with the family.

Develop the habit of engaging in relationship as your family begins the day. Introduce the idea of noticing and affirming each other as simply as saying, "Good morning!" Consider each other's needs as you share a bathroom or eat breakfast together. Let breakfast prep and cleanup be about caring about each other instead of keeping score or justifying selfishness with "It's not my turn!"

We all wake up with God-given needs for affirmation, acceptance, and servant love. When children start the day having these needs met, and meeting those needs for others, they're starting their day with integrity rather than as slaves to their emotions. A relationally mature morning routine is a gift that keeps on giving—for a lifetime.

Share the work of the home.

Working alongside Mom, Dad, or an older sibling to meet the needs of the home, family, yard, neighbors, and neighborhood is a vital experience for young children.

It is the part of the journey that reminds them **childhood is preparation for adulthood, not prolonged adolescence.**

Learning to use a sharp knife, an oven, a lawn mower, and a dishwasher are more life-giving than learning to use the remote for the TV or the apps on a phone. Children experience impact and influence for good in a big world when they help cook dinner, mow the yard, work in the garden, or chop down a tree. Vacuuming, cleaning, and doing laundry are all part of living life as a family member, instead of as a guest in a hotel. Children learn who they are when we give them responsibilities that remind them of their true identity.

Deep satisfaction is not found in a life ill-equipped, or the habit of thinking only about ourselves. Not equipped to live a responsible life, children carry the weight of their own immaturity. There is no more natural cure for entitlement than the real thrill of blessing others. "I do because I care," is a true statement about a child of God.

Develop a broad range of leisure skills and interests.

Only trustworthy experiences offer our children health and peace because such experiences are consistent with—rather than in conflict with—God's design for their lives. Affections for good, true, and beautiful are caught, not taught. As with fine wine, we acquire a taste for mature living ... or we don't. When home is a place of love and inspiration, our children will have a place to linger, rest, and find restoration. These are the gifts of leisure.

The activities of leisure are often the kind that require an adult's help—at least to get started. Wood carving, weaving, leather work, sculpting, needlework, knitting, crocheting, and baking are just a few opportunities for handwork. Fishing, hunting, and gardening offer opportunities to enjoy fresh air and sunshine, and to breathe.

Nature study invites children to develop a lifelong relationship with all of creation. Picture study invites us to play with color and hue, texture and light. Composer study offers both rest and inspiration—in the gift of music that has endured for generations. Artists and composers become our friends. We learn to enjoy museums and symphonies because we have a relationship with the people who have given us the gifts of art and music.

Share the experience of good books.

Reading is not a subject at school; reading is relationship.

Books offer children friendships with people and places and ideas and words. As parents and grandparents, we have the responsibility of protecting children from toxic relationships and providing them with only the best experiences with the best books. **Giving a child a crummy book is giving him a crummy mentor.**

The best books need to first be read aloud. We get this privilege! We get to give the gift of authentic literature to our children and introduce them to a world they can only receive and enjoy as we help them learn to navigate words on a page. Children find confidence in experiencing a bigger world in stories from far and wide. And our nearness contributes to the relational aspect of reading—while we offer the gift of soul-settling memories.

It's vital that we don't make reading about performing or earning points. When reading is about achievement, children count pages as a way of proving their skill—or they fear their struggle. Earning takes the space where loving belongs. Love is patient. Love keeps no record of wrongs. Reading is not a way of earning, it is a way of living.

Learning to read is as valuable to a child as learning to walk. Some babies learn to walk when they are nine or ten months old. Some learn to walk when they are 15 or 16 months old. The timetable for learning to read is unpredictable, too. Fear of being "behind" makes reading more difficult. Reading together protects real struggle from shame.

Oh, the freedom to enjoy the world of good books in their leisure! This is the gift of reading.

Play games together.

Games offer opportunities to wait their turn, develop skills, recognize patterns and consequences, problem-solve, and experience a wide range of emotions. Celebrations punctuate the full thrill of victory. Conversations help process unpleasant emotions after the agony of defeat. Like counting the silverware needed to set the table, counting the dots on dice is a math lesson for a young child. Rolling more than one die gives a need to add and moving a game piece gives practice with one-to-one correspondence and counting.

Because board games are played together, mistakes are discovered quickly. Moving five spaces instead of six is corrected *without penalty or shame.* Dealing six cards instead of seven gets resolved rather than graded. Children will clue into either our patience or our anxiety if they struggle with numbers. They'll know what we're thinking if they "take too long" to count the dice, or the dots on the dominoes.

Playing games is an opportunity to offer the vital gift of affirmation, instead of self-doubt. "You're learning. I believe in you" is a gift of love.

"What story are you telling yourself right now?" is a priceless conversation, too.

Enjoy play and rest.

Children need fresh air and sunshine. They need chances to run and jump and spin in circles. They need to balance and skip and throw sticks and gather wildflowers. Blocks and dolls and dress-up and tag are all components of a trustworthy childhood. Red Rover and London Bridge and Duck, Duck, Goose are more than just fun.

Rest is vital, too.

Screen time is not the kind of rest or play our children's bodies need. Screen time is entertainment, not child's play. And the sights and sounds don't allow the mind and body the rest it needs from constant stimulation. A parent's love can offer children the protection they need to enjoy both times of unstructured play and peaceful rest.

Be intentional about habit formation.

Immature habits deny many children, and adults alike, the full and free life we are created to enjoy. Mature habits support our relationships and move us in the direction of our dreams. Immature habits cause injury in our relationships and can keep us from living in the delight of our destiny.

Habits are formed in childhood. Immature habits of carelessness affect more than just the condition of our children's bedrooms, or the way they chew their food. The habit of carelessness affects the work children do during school, too. And this is good news. A mature habit of carefulness affects bedrooms, table manners, and school work as well.

Helping children develop mature habits is the fruit of intentional, coordinated effort between the parent and the child. The immature habit is not a source of conflict—rather, it is a shared concern. The resolution of the weakness is a shared priority. It's not about fixing. Developing helpful habits is a part of growing up.

The habit of giving focused attention is vital in the life of a young scholar. More importantly, this habit is vital in personal relationships. **Giving attention is a mature habit. Not giving attention is an immature habit.** This perspective—seeing the inability to give focused attention as a habit that has yet to be developed—gives our children great hope. We can change our habits. It will take time, commitment, and effort—and the fruit of this investment will be invaluable.

Imagine 100 young children on the first day of school. Fifty children line up on one side of the playground, and fifty children line up across the field. They are lining up to play catch. On the first day, only about ten of the children will be able to throw the ball far enough and accurately enough for another child to really catch it. Many children will be new to the skill of catching. If this skill is the focus of our time, energy, and intentionality, 99% of the children will be able to throw and catch successfully before the end of the school year.

Skill is habit well formed. Attention is similar to catching and throwing. When we help children, the habit will develop naturally. This work is personal, more than clinical. Some children will develop the skill in a few days, some a few weeks. For some it will take months, or a few years. When we begin this work when our children are young, the immature habit has not yet formed a deep and formidable rut.

Create an environment that supports success.

Parents expecting a newborn baby take great care in setting up a nursery. As our children grow up, they continue to benefit from our care and attention to the details in their rooms and the environment in our homes. Clutter is a distraction. It doesn't remind us who we are.

Help your child de-clutter their room. Talk to your child about when they're ready to trade the train table or the doll house for a desk. Make intentional decisions about televisions and computer games in children's bedrooms. Screens rarely lend our children strength or offer them what they need to grow up. Sometimes saying "no" is the best way we can love our children well.

Build emotional fluency.

Emotions add great flavor and texture to life. They make life both enjoyable and uncomfortable. Helping our children deal maturely with their emotions is as vital as teaching them to handle fire and water with intentional care. Without ways of "getting it out," our children will have no choice but to live them out.

Fiery emotions can explode in our face. Others can flood our homes.

Children need a generous vocabulary to talk about how they feel. Frustrated is different than angry. Nervous is not the same as afraid.

It comes naturally for us to teach our children what to do and not to do with a hot stove, an electrical outlet, and a baseball bat. We can teach what to do and not to do with emotions, too. Emotions are meant to be experienced and processed, not denied, stuffed, or kept hidden.

Dealing maturely with our emotions includes helping our children recognize that joy is our normal state. When I'm sad, it's good to be me here with you. When I'm excited, it's good to be me here with you. Joy is always the way God feels in relationship with us. Our children benefit from experiencing this truth.

Returning to joy—or rebounding—from every unpleasant emotion is the foundation for emotional health. Getting stuck in unpleasant emotions leads to anxiety and depression. When our children are angry, we can help them experience their anger, get it out in words or art or exercise, and then return to the inner peace that is joy. When they are sad, we have the privilege of comforting them, and helping them believe the truth about themselves and the circumstances.

Often, returning to joy means teaching our children about the power of forgiveness, and of rebuilding trust. Children who risk connecting in trusting relationships build the joy-strength real life is going to require.

Our children can live from the truth of their new identity when they learn that emotions don't belong in the driver's seat of life. Emotions are important passengers, but they don't get to be in charge of our decisions. Other people's emotions don't either. Our behavior comes from what we value and what we believe to be true. Feelings sometimes lie. Unpleasant emotions are our clue to connect in relationships of trust. Love will give us the strength to make decisions intentionally, instead of emotionally.

By design, maturity will come. Maturity brings care—and a full life in a big world. We can offer this world—for the children's sake.

Chapter Eight
Where Do We
Begin with Older
Children?

I met Isaiah when he was fifteen. I would have hired him to care for any of our grandchildren; I would have voted for him for President. Isaiah carried himself with a quiet strength, and a calmness that invited trust. His vocabulary was that of an avid reader. But he couldn't read.

Dyslexia had shut down the freeways that were supposed to take this young man on grand adventures. The pathways in his brain had almost visible road signs that declared: "Construction ahead. Expect delays."

Dyslexia had been only one of many labels on a list when Isaiah was young. The diagnosis from the doctor had not been the words any parent wants to hear. Almost ten years later, trust and love had already turned most of his significant struggles into strengths. His parents had worked hard and loved well. Isaiah had trusted hard. But dyslexia had kept a tight grip.

As a high school student, all of his books still had to be read aloud to him—or he listened to audio editions.

Writing was like laboring through a dark jungle. Spelling tangles wrapped around his words, keeping them hidden, along with his hope.

Isaiah's mom and I were new friends. We'd met at church. Over coffee one day she asked if I thought I could help. "I'd love to try," I replied.

I agreed to meet with Isaiah one hour a day, two days a week, for six weeks. After that, we agreed I would better understand the size of the tangle and we'd be able to make a long-term plan.

Isaiah and I spent half of our time reading together *Dandelion Wine* by Ray Bradbury. It was an assignment for his high school literature class. The other half of our time was spent transcribing the book of James.

Our reading followed along this way: I read a sentence, then Isaiah reread the same sentence. I read another sentence; he read it, too. At the end of a paragraph, I'd read all the sentences together. He'd read them after me. If he misread a word, I'd ask him to read it again—correctly. I knew we were untangling his brain. I knew we were building new roads, and the new roads needed to be trustworthy.

A few weeks into our time together, Isaiah said something like this: "Janet, I feel hopeful because it seems like I'm making progress. But it feels like I'm cheating."

"Why do you feel like you're cheating, Isaiah?"

"Because you're telling me what the words are," he said.

"Oh, Isaiah! I am so sorry. I am so sorry that your experience in education has taught you that helping is cheating. Jesus will always tell you what the words are. Right now, you just need Jesus with skin on," I said.

The weak become strong.

As the weeks continued, I could read entire paragraphs for Isaiah to repeat. Soon he was able to repeat whole pages without error. As his confidence and reading maturity became more evident, we spent some of our reading time letting him read the text on his own. When he ran out of capacity for independent reading, we'd return to the echo reading pattern. Isaiah trusted my help.

Love is the construction chemical in our brains. Isaiah was building new roads in his mind in all the ways he was responding in trust.

Transcribing is simply copying. It is a powerful experience in the way it invites students to experience the ideas in great writing at a lingering pace. **What echo reading offers in the experience of a good book, transcribing offers in the experience of a great writer.** Students copy beautiful words intentionally arranged in strong paragraphs. They copy correct spelling, punctuation marks, and use of capital and lowercase letters. Isaiah needed these experiences.

If you had wandered into the dining room when Isaiah and I were transcribing together, you would have seen us sitting side by side, each with a Bible, a journal, and a pencil. I was transcribing, too. You would have heard me read a Scripture verse aloud, and Isaiah repeat the words as he read it. Then you would have heard me saying each word, and giving instructions to use capital or lowercase letters, and spelling each word—one letter at a time.

Isaiah needed this kind of support. And he never sensed from me that this level of support was a concern or a bother to me. My tone of voice and body language did not communicate frustration or judgment in any way. Nothing in the experience communicated he was "behind." His struggle did not disrupt my joy. I was at peace helping him learn. My love was protecting him from shame.

After we finished writing one sentence, Isaiah would read the sentence aloud on his own, and we would repeat the same steps as we both transcribed the next sentence. When we finished transcribing James, chapter one, Isaiah read the chapter aloud, with 100% accuracy. We recorded it on my phone. The recording was the first time his mother heard him reading Scripture of any substantial length independently. Love was having its effect.

Five weeks into our initial six-week agreement, I received a text from Isaiah's mom. The text read: "I am texting this in tears. I just walked by the living room and saw Isaiah lying on the couch reading *The Hobbit.*"

"Count it all joy, my brothers, when you meet trials of various kinds, for you know that the testing of your faith produces steadfastness. And let steadfastness have its full effect, that you may be perfect and complete, lacking in nothing," James 1: 2-4, ESV.

I share this story about Isaiah in a chapter offering ideas about transformational education with older students because it is a picture of real confusion—and real learning.

This is our calling as educators, with children of all ages. Help them untangle. Equip them in the ways of trust and "Follow me." Remember the power of working "with," rather than having students work "for" us—or for the motive of earning a grade.

Attention is a function of maturity and habit.

We learn to give focused attention in relationships with people who help us trust what God says is true about us, especially when we experience emotional or academic struggle. When children do not experience help when they struggle, the fear and shame they feel is a side effect of the flow of cortisol in their system. Fear shuts down the immune system and all systems associated with growing. Maturity is put on hold when we're anxious or afraid.

Giving focused attention is a mature habit. The struggle to give focused attention may be very, very real—much like the struggle to learn to walk. And it is a struggle that has great hope for resolution when our children give us permission to lend them strength.

What does lending them strength look like, practically speaking? It means we have honest and peaceful conversations about the immature habits that may be contributing to the problem with giving attention. Proper hydration is vital for the mind to focus. Some research suggests 95% of most ADHD symptoms would be resolved if children simply drank enough water. Nutrition is vital, too. Our bodies and brains work on the fuel we consume. Building neurological pathways depends on a healthy and nutritious diet.

Older children also need rest. Vital rest depends on schedules that respect this real need, and a willingness in the child to trust the need for sleep more than the need to stay plugged in to technology.

In an academic environment, children need someone they trust to help them develop the habit of giving focused attention. In a large classroom, this means sitting close to the teacher, and responding appropriately every time the teacher redirects inattention. In a smaller setting, this means sitting side by side more often than across the table. A child of any age must trust "I am for you" from the parent or teacher.

When any academic or behavior struggle becomes an issue in relationship, good performance becomes the means to reconnect. Performance-dependent relationships are fear-based relationships; fear is one of the causes of ADHD, not the cure.

To recognize the cause is to have hope for a resolution—and a cure. Because we believe in a cure for cancer or heart disease, we can also give our children hope for a cure for conditions that impair mental health. ADHD is not a forever diagnosis. We can share this hope with our children. Struggles are real, and hope is real, too.

Intentionally invest time—and ask for help.

In this life, time is a finite gift. Unlike money, we don't have an opportunity to make more time if we waste it. I sometimes wonder why we are greatly offended when our kids waste money, and we almost don't seem to notice when they waste time. **What a legacy we can give our children when we offer the perspective that time is a treasure, and it can be invested in ways that pay richly in relationships.**

Relationships lend us strength when we are brave enough to choose humility, instead of pretending. **Hiding wastes time.** This is not a lesson our children will learn from their peers or on social media. But they can learn it from us.

We get to model vulnerability in our homes. We get to spend time in honest conversations, not defending ourselves or blaming others, but asking for help when we struggle. When we are confident in who God says we are, our identity isn't at stake. The only thing we have to lose is more time in an old rut. As our children watch us experience safety and personal growth, they'll consider building a habit of humility and asking for help.

Safe places to struggle are safe places to grow. We can teach our children to invest time, not just in the places they are strong, but in the places that they're weak. If reading is a struggle, we can plan time to sit side by side and share the load that will lighten in the long run. If math seems like a foreign language, we can schedule time together to translate and help untangle the operations. Spending time together redeems weaknesses and strengthens relationships.

Healthy—instead of toxic—vulnerability

Maturity doesn't happen in immature or toxic relationships. Consider middle school. Putting hundreds of 13- and 14-year-olds under the same roof without a very high percentage of mature people to trust and depend on is a relatively new idea in our country—and it's not a helpful one.

A peer group is not a community. In a peer group, there's no one with more experience who is willing and able to sacrificially care for the well-being of the group—or for the weak. The weak don't become strong; they stay vulnerable.

In a performance-obsessed culture, the best outcome a young person can hope for is the accomplishment of "I am better than you." It's why some immature drivers race to get ahead of all the others, like a young child running to get to the head of the line. This lie sometimes comes out as "At least I'm more popular than you." Social media friends and followers can attach themselves to this vulnerability in toxic ways.

If being first isn't an option, "At least I'm not the worst" becomes the standard for belonging. There's not much protection from these immature ways of relating in a peer group, so the culture unintentionally teaches our children to segregate and be selfish, instead of to depend on others in trustworthy ways.

"Love one another" becomes a community service project rather than the way one young person connects with another who can't seem to find a place to belong. Distracted by earning points during childhood, teenagers don't have the maturity to notice the needs of others. Compliance replaces kindness—and common courtesy.

On social media, a performance-obsessed peer culture urges our children to be the riskiest, rather than the most reliable. Instead of the strong helping the weak, the weak become the most vulnerable. Fight-or-flight responses can look like bullying—or suicide.

In a maturity-oriented culture, the strong care for the weak—who become the strong who care for the weak. In a healthy culture, children learn who God says they are, independent of their accomplishments or their struggles. Vulnerability opens the door to grace, and trusting this grace resolves their immature issues. Children then offer this grace to others, too.

A few practical suggestions for pre-teens and teenagers: Prioritize opportunities for children of all ages to spend in multi-generational communities. Spending a few weeks with grandparents in the summer may be one option. Sharing meals together as a family is a good option, too.

Encourage your teenager to get a part-time job as a babysitter or a mother's helper. Establish an environment of grace in your home that encourages siblings to help each other with homework or with getting ready in the mornings. Encourage your older teen to volunteer at a memory care facility or in the children's ministry at church.

Maturity is as natural as breathing, unless the process gets hijacked by toxic relationships. Our children can know and recognize the hijackers—and ask for help, when they trust us.

Read good books together.

Great literature invites conversations about integrity and honor, shame and fear, love and hope, strength and valor. The conversations are as vital as the act of reading.

Young adults will choose to read good books on their own if they've been led into the world of worthy literacy. The covers of most great books read during the teenage years are opened because a teacher invited a young adult to risk an investment of their time and effort, and because they shared the journey together.

Lingering long enough to notice the author's talent in a particular word choice or sentence structure is like noticing the after-taste of high quality chocolate.

Pondering motive and considering the way the author structures the climax with sustained suspense are invitations to consider the craft of a well-written story.

Paragraphs and essays are a natural by-product of mature conversations. Students don't simply write to complete an assignment. They are following the footsteps of great authors and are becoming writers, too. In friendships with great authors, readers experience a natural urge to respond.

If reading is inhaling, writing is exhaling. Young adults become fluent writers with focused practice and trusted feedback. Students find their voice—and have something to say. They learn to put their own words on the page and offer inspiration that begs for a response from the reader as well.

Dependable, not independent

I wonder if, as Americans, we're confused about independence. I sometimes think we've tangled up the Declaration of Independence with the "pull yourself up by your boot straps" mentality and have invented some toxic version of "at least I'm better than you" melting pot soup.

In its infancy, the American Dream was about the freedom to live with great hope, without the prejudices of a communist, socialist, or monarchist caste system. The original American Dream was about building a healthy community in freedom, rather than in oppression.

The Declaration of Independence was the healthy cry of a newborn nation that said, "No!" when old England wanted to bolster her own strength at the expense of the young colonies. Recognizing America's immaturity as measured in years, the Founding Fathers built safe-guards to protect the integrity of the new Republic.

The checks and balances in the judiciously crafted United States' Constitution established a system that remains anything but a model of independence. Each branch of government *depends on* the other two branches—to be trustworthy and *dependable,* so the country as a whole is trustworthy and *dependable* for its citizens, and for the world.

What if we had a similar constitution—as a parent or a grandparent? What if we modeled a life for children that helped them live dependent on trustworthy relationships, too? When children humbly depend on God and others, they grow up to be trustworthy and dependable, not independent in the ways that leave them vulnerable and immature.

They will live this life if we do; this can be the culture at home. **Mature relationships protect our children's hope to live free from the tyranny of their own imma-turity.** Depending on and protected by a trustworthy community opens wide the doors to our children's unique dreams—and leaves the doors open for the dreams of their children, too.

Develop affections for what God gives us to love.

God is the parent who continually prepares a feast of nutritious food, and sometimes we can be the child who is a distracted, picky eater. Meeting our felt needs does not satisfy our real needs. We can be overweight—and starving for nutrition, when we don't trust what God offers us in love.

We can help our children *experience God's love* in the real world. Love offers us all we need, that we cannot earn. We are offered safety in the boundlessness of God's creativity. I remember living in the hill country of Texas and thinking, "If God can create all of this, He can create a way for me to navigate my current struggles." I wouldn't have had that thought if I hadn't been in the middle of beautiful—if I had been in the middle of the mall, instead of in the middle of the hills.

We are offered affirmation in God's Word. We can offer our children a relationship with Scripture that is love, not law. Nature offers us the gift of love that is significance. "If God notices and cares for the tiniest plants and animals, I can trust Him to notice and care for me, too."

New life that comes after pain—or trauma—offers us God's committed love. God is faithful to work all things together for good (Romans 8:28). We can witness His love in the miracle of birth, after hours of painful labor. We can notice the power of restorative love in the fresh green springing up from the tired earth after a forest fire. We can rest in the rhythms of grace when we notice the patterns and predictability of day and night, summer and winter, hurt and healing.

Our children will not experience the newness of life unless we share the miracles—of newborn babies, rosebuds, cherry blossoms, and puppies! Our children's eyes may miss the green sprigs in the blackness of the burned-out forest. They may find winter hopeless if we don't remind them of the coming spring. The life we lead, and the words we use to talk about the life we have, will either attract our children to God's faithful love—or to something less.

Nothing can separate us from the love of God, and our children will not experience His love if they are trying to earn it—or if they are distracted by lesser things. What we invest from all that God grants us in this life becomes our legacy and testimony. Everything else will fade away.

"The question is not,—how much does the youth know? when he has finished his education—but how much does he care? and about how many orders of things does he care? In fact, how large is the room in which he finds his feet set? and, therefore, how full is the life he has before him?"
~ *Charlotte Mason, "School Education"*

Chapter Nine
Traditions by Design

When Doug and I first started enjoying dinner together, his 4,500 square foot house had been on the market for almost two years. Realtors showed potential buyers through the property at least seven or eight times every week. The feedback was always positive—and no one had yet offered a contract. In almost two years!

By the time we were excited about getting married, we were more than ready to sell the house. We didn't need that much space. All five of our children were already grown and had families of their own. The home was going to be too big of an empty nest, and we wanted a fresh start.

We prayed and prayed, asking God to help us by sending the perfect buyer. Potential buyers continued to tour the property, no fewer than five times a week. Still, no offers.

So we offered up a different prayer. "God, we admit we don't want to keep this house. And we admit this, too. What we really want is to trust You—and Your plans for us and our family. Please make Your plans clear to us. We want to follow Your lead. Please help us know what to do. Amen."

Silence. No more calls from realtors. Not one more showing of the house. After a few weeks, we trusted—and took the house off the market. We got married, and I moved in. We painted the downstairs. The fresh paint made it seem more like our home. We were confused—and honestly, disappointed. And we were trusting God.

Three months into our new marriage, it became obvious that Doug's dad—then 86 years old and struggling with stage 4 kidney disease—was no longer able to care for himself independently. He needed help, and someone to share meals with and have conversation. He needed to stop driving!

Doug and I moved upstairs. His dad moved into our master bedroom. The master bathroom had a walk-in shower. "Big, big Papa"—as he was affectionately called—could maneuver the downstairs, and we had more than enough room upstairs. God knew.

The adventures of sharing our home with him lasted until early July. He passed away about six months after becoming our housemate.

By this time, we had become new friends with two talented interior designers. Both lived in Fort Worth. They wanted the house to sell, too, because they were praying we'd move north from the Houston area. These two friends drove down on a Sunday afternoon, just a few days after Big, big Papa moved to heaven. They wanted to help us stage our house because we were ready to put it back on the market.

Monday morning, there was a knock at the door. One of our friends had hired movers to come and rearrange all of our furniture. In response to the "emergency" of Doug's dad's failing health, we had moved some things upstairs that belonged downstairs. We'd moved some things to the garage. The house looked more like some kind of care facility instead of a home for a big family with enough kids to fill the bedrooms.

Within 24 hours, the house looked like a beautiful, well planned, thoughtfully arranged, and tastefully decorated home. It sold in eight days—for a considerably higher price than we had been asking for more than two years. God knew.

I offer this story in a chapter about "Traditions by Design" because today's education system doesn't have many. The traditions we rely on today are left over from a response to emergency—in the 1950s. Many things are upside down. Our traditions are false traditions—developed in default.

The crisis of the baby boom is now long past. Our attempts to standardize education, in an attempt perhaps to right a sinking ship, are not serving our children well. The immaturity crisis our nation is experiencing—along with staggering statistics about young people crippled with addiction, anxiety, depression, loneliness, and suicide—leave us no choice but to "hire a moving crew" and put schools together again in a way that serves children by design, not default.

New traditions, practices, and ways of relating

Every intentional tradition, practice, and way of relating at school can offer children transformational learning. We can offer love, not fear. We can help children struggle well in truth in ways that give them the strength to work through confusion and celebrate real learning.

We can invite love to invade the atmosphere at school with true ideas from books, the beauty of music and nature—and with the care we take to create a schedule and a way of being together that is for the children's sake.

Three intentional traditions on this new road in education that support student maturity are:

- multi-age student groupings,
- school schedules that respect real needs—and offer time for play and rest,
- and a broad and rigorous curriculum.

More than simply writing about these truths, I've been offering them to families for a few years now. Many of the parents currently risking education by design are offering a John 15 Academy education to their children. John 15 Academy is an educational entity—and our 501(c)3. I am honored to serve as a trusted guide to this group of world changers.

Turning educational history on this hinge—to build schools by design and offer children new hope—is my life's dream. I am a pioneer, perhaps—a sort of "Christopher Columbus" in the world of education. This book serves as a foundational resource for fellow pioneers. I offer you these specific and intentional traditions on the pages of this book, based on my research and experience about what children really need.

Instead of age-based grade levels, John 15 Academy designates five "Schools" for students, based on academic needs, and relational maturity. Because of the flexibility provided by the number of years offered in each School, children can spend as much—or as little—time as needed, to build the maturity that supports academic performance. Children are not labeled as "ahead" or "behind."

Primary School (students attend for 1-2 years)
Elementary School for Young Children (students attend for 1-2 years)
Elementary School for Older Children (students attend for 3-4 years)
Intermediate School (students attend for 3-4 years)
High School (students attend for 4-5 years)

Whether a child spends the minimum or maximum number of years in each School, curriculum choices are made so that a child experiences new reading selections in each subject every year. Math instruction is student-specific, rather than "grade-level" specific. Science instruction in High School is student-specific, as well.

Additional information about the schedules for each School, and some of the fundamental convictions that guide instruction for children in each group are offered in Appendix B.

The practice of narration

If you are familiar with Charlotte Mason, you are familiar with narration. I almost hope you aren't familiar, yet. It may be easier to explain the practice of narration as a fresh idea, rather than restore the practice, if narration has been an experience of pain or fear or dread.

Like the beauty of the Gospel, we can too often make law out of love. Some schools have made laws about narration. It too often comes with performance standards. Can I protect you from these standards? **Narration is like exhaling. It is simply giving back after you have received.**

Imagine sharing a funny story with a friend about something that happened with your spouse. Think about calling your mom and telling her the story of the baseball game or the ballet recital that she didn't get to attend. Narration is the way young children learn the power of story. It is also a way they can offer something mature in conversation. Because they have received, they can now give.

The natural experience of narration follows like this: First, children enjoy a well-chosen book. Then the teacher says, "Tell back the part about the struggle." Or, "Tell back the part at the beginning of the chapter." One child responds; the other children listen and offer more details.

Narrating in a group is like a progressive dinner. Each person adds a part of the meal. Children eventually learn to narrate on their own, including significant details, in the correct sequence, and with much of the author's language. Offering a complete and mature narration of this kind takes time and practice, like cooking a gourmet dinner. If children are required to do more before they are ready, they will respond in fear instead of trust. It will become something they dread, instead of a way of engaging in conversation.

The experience of a good book is an opportunity for all of us to sit at the feet of an artist. The artist is the author. Carefully chosen books for children offer vivid experiences. The vocabulary in each story becomes a color palette. Each child learns to paint with words. Because narration is an exercise in Literature and Bible and History and Science (and any subject offered from a written text), children become fluent in the language of many subjects. They feel natural with new words. Because it isn't paint by number, narrating is often messy at first. The experience is very different from completing a worksheet or answering questions at the end of the chapter.

Unlike an assignment, the experience of narration is for the benefit of the child. It is not for the purpose of completing a task, staying busy, or getting a grade. Narration is about relationship, with people and with books. For children, it offers the experience of a mature conversation with real substance. It is an invitation to grow up.

An experience—not a race

Because real life traumas (illness, divorce of parents, natural disasters, death of a family member...) come uninvited in children's lives, the flexibility offered by the five Schools encourages children to heal from such traumas, as needed—without any added stress or fear of "failing" a grade level.

Multi-age groupings encourage dialogue and collaboration—both of which are vital to supporting maturity. These groupings also invite children to both learn from and lend strength to their peers. Instead of synchronized steps through standardized curriculum, students experience the love that meets their needs, celebrates their successes, and lends them strength in their weaknesses—especially in the ways brave love disconnects struggle from shame. Students offer this love to each other, too.

A generous and rigorous curriculum offers a big world to our children. The curriculum is generous because children are invited to "taste and see"—and develop appetites for a wide range of life-giving subjects. Children experience personal significance finding their unique place in a big world, not striving to outperform their classmates in a small one. The curriculum is rigorous because life if rigorous.

We do children a disservice when we offer them pre-digested subjects so they can score 100% in every subject/every day. Real life does not come to us in pre-digested packages. As adults and parents, we are not required to score 100% in laundry and budgeting and cooking and work-life balancing. Why do we burden our children with this stress?

The healing power of "with"
When our children are infants, we live life together. Our love meets their needs and they get stronger. Because they're growing up, they're also learning. We don't show them a flash card with the word "ma-ma." We speak to them—and show our obvious delight we they begin to work hard at finding their voice. More than "teaching" them, we are loving them—and living life with them.

We affirm and encourage. We notice and get excited. We give babies our full attention—and we help them.

Babies don't do work "for" us, they follow our lead. As toddlers, they work "with" us—in the kitchen, and in the yard or in the garden.

Living life together, there is great hope—for growing up, and the learning that comes naturally with maturity.

Reading "with' our children is vital—more than asking them to read "for" us. When we sit with a child and invite them to "follow me" into a good story, we are doing so much more than "teaching" them to read. We are connecting with them, and sharing something of value that we love. Oxytocin is flowing freely—and it is not hard for our children to trust and receive.

And if reading—or math, or giving focused attention—is a struggle for them one day, living life together is often the best therapy. Struggling in safe relationships offers many opportunities to connect—in trust and love, not fear and shame.

So many times, healing and growth take place while a child is experiencing real life—pulling weeds *together,* or folding laundry, or washing the car—or the dishes. It is in these moments of working *with* a trusted adult that they experience the maturity and healing they desperately need in math or reading or to develop the habit of attention or perseverance.

The practical work of real life offers a beautiful untangling. They remember who they are. "I am a son." "I am a daughter." "I belong." "I am growing up." "I am learning."

What happens in their hearts restores order to the chaos in their minds. "Do not conform any longer to the pattern of the world, but be transformed by the renewing of your mind," Romans 12:2, ESV. As parents and teachers, we get to play a sacred part in this miracle of transformation in our children's lives.

As our children experience real life alongside us, they experience significance. Experiencing significance is experiencing love. Love heals and untangles the pathways in our brains. Love builds new connections. Sometimes, without working on the issues, we discover the issues are resolved.

Education by design offers a new treatment protocol: relationship. When our children stay connected in relationships that meet their God-given needs—and that help them in their places of weakness—love literally makes learning possible.

Good questions pair well with great books.

Looking closely at false traditions requires us to consider the ways we ask young adults to respond to great books. Writing book reports or answering the questions at the end of a chapter can feel like poor service at a fine restaurant, while trying to enjoy an exquisite meal. The quality of the interaction with the story must match the value of the book. Mature conversations are key.

Mature conversations are about ideas more often than facts. Questions have more than one right answer. The kinds of questions offered by design are different than the questions we're used to answering by default.

These questions are offered as examples. The list is not given to students as an assignment. They are used to guide discussion. One or two questions may be offered as a writing prompt.

By design, good questions are offered as a gift to students—to help them see life more clearly. Questions can offer a path to truth, and a way of wrestling with it and digesting it.

For the purpose of example here, I have inserted the names of Hester Prynne, Pearl, the Reverend Arthur Dimmesdale, and Roger Chillingworth from *The Scarlet Letter*. The questions can be adapted and used with any good book. Most lessons would only include the consideration of one or a few of these questions at a time, not all.

1. **What is** <u>Rev. Dimmesdale</u> **believing to be true right now about himself? What is he believing to be true about his friend/foe? What is he believing to be true about God? How do we know?** (Remember: Behavior is the mirror of belief.)

2. **What is** <u>Roger Chillingworth's</u> **motive? What evidence do we find of this motive?**

3. **What is** <u>Roger</u> **afraid of? What is the evidence and the effect of this fear in his own life? What is the effect of his fear on** <u>Hester?</u> **On** <u>Rev. Dimmesdale?</u>

4. **What is the impact and influence of shame on** <u>Rev. Dimmesdale?</u> **What is the source of his shame? In what ways is shame evident?**

5. **What is the impact and influence of love on** <u>Hester?</u> **Who/what is the source of love? In what ways is love evident?**

6. **What do we know about** <u>Roger Chillingworth?</u> **What do we know about his integrity?**

7. **What is** <u>Roger's</u> **impact and influence on** <u>Hester?</u> **What is** <u>Rev. Dimmesdale's</u> **impact and influence**

on Hester? Where is hope in the story? Where is hopelessness?

8. How does Hester respond to the wrong she commits?

9. What does the relationship with Pearl offer Hester? What does the relationship cost her?

10. How do we know that Hester cares about the well-being of Pearl? OR How do we know that Hester doesn't care about the well-being of Pearl?

11. Consider Roger and Arthur's relationship. Is it a relationship of freedom? Are both free to say "yes" and "no" in this relationship? What evidence do we find in the story of this freedom? (or evidence of fear, or codependency?)

12. What is the impact and influence of Pearl's relationship with Rev. Dimmesdale on Hester?

13. Consider Hester. What is the evidence of his/her habit of diligence? (OR habit of attention to detail, habit of considering others before him/herself, habit of exaggerating/minimizing, habit of truthfulness, habit of paying attention, habit of listening, habit of not listening, habit of carelessness, habit of blaming,...)

14. How does Hester's relationship with Pearl offer her strength and protection?

15. Who does Pearl trust? What is evidence of this trust?

Transformational education offers life.

Imagine the first day of college for students having experienced education by design. The young adult is confident in their academic preparations, and comfortable asking for help when it is needed. The college freshman seeks out relationships of trust on campus with professors and new friends. **When emotions attempt to hijack behavior, the mature young adult recognizes the circumstances for what they are and leans heavily on a strong foundation of personal values and convictions.**

Imagine the first year of married life for young adults having more than a good GPA to carry across the threshold of a first home. Imagine the life of young parents... and a brand new generation growing up on a road, now less new... and more well-traveled. Next to the "What to Expect From Your One Year Old" book on the shelf, there is a well-worn, dogged-eared family heirloom: *Education By Design, Not Default: How Brave Love Creates Fearless Learning.*

"My Beloved—Come to Me as a needy child,
and I will send you to the world as an equipped adult."
~ Steve Eden

Chapter Ten
Curriculum by
Design

The history of American education is a history of purpose. Public education is publicly funded education. The government pays to create experiences for children that it trusts will meet the needs—and establish the well-being—of the country.

In the relatively short history of the United States of America, public education has served many purposes. Most of the purposes of public education are political. When I typed that last sentence, I had two thoughts: (1) Of course. Public schools are supported by government money. And, (2) Oh my! Google offers this definition of politics: "the activities associated with the governance of a country, especially the debate or conflict among individuals or parties having or hoping to achieve power."

If you're recognizing an agenda in the arena of education, feel free. The agenda is intentional. The history of education is the history of the purpose of those in power—or desiring to be in power.

This look back in history in a chapter about "Curriculum by Design" is not written with an intent to arouse alarm. It is written with the intent to arouse a greater intention. Curriculum is always chosen to achieve the purpose of education.

What if education offers society more than a docile and compliant work force? What if education offers children more than a good job? What if education offers more than a way of maintaining or gaining power for any one particular political agenda?

Education funded by the government for the sake of the well-being of the country is upside down. Because it's upside-down, it's dysfunctional. Imagine expecting good results when using a funnel upside-down. Functional education is about what the children need—instead of what the economy needs.

When we meet the needs of the children, the economy will explode because children will grow up with more energy to work, and they will bring more creativity rather than basic conformity. The future of the country will be better served when education, funded by the government—or funded by private schools or in schools at home, is for the sake of the well-being of the children.

When adults sacrifice for the sake of the children, children grow up and become adults who also sacrifice for the sake of helping children grow up. Growing up is about a great deal more than being good and passing tests. Meeting the needs of children is a better way to meet the needs of the country and establish the well-being of the world. Education can offer students an honest childhood, and in doing so offer the world trustworthy adults.

Untangling false traditions about curriculum

The real world is not an easy world. Life's lessons do not often come to children in pre-measured, age-appropriate bites. It is a false tradition to offer curriculum from a children's menu, and wisdom does not ignore real needs. Childhood can be an apprenticeship at a banquet of good and true and beautiful. Love disconnects struggle from shame. It doesn't disconnect struggle from truth.

Children benefit when we help them navigate big ideas and real struggles, one trusting moment at a time. Instead of requiring them daily to color in tiny squares in a graph paper sized life, love invites children onto a blank canvas—full of risks and challenges, with opportunities for intimacy and creativity, and big spaces for bundles of energy. The needs of others in a big world invite a child's impact and influence for good.

Life is an adventure, not a race. Children may experience real delays, but they are not behind. They may experience the blessing of ease and efficiency, and they are not ahead. Every moment of every day, every child is right on time. The only thing that truly limits children is their choice to trust love—or something less.

When we make curriculum choices for children prioritized by emotion, ease, or economy—we encourage them to live life in these self-limiting ways, too. Children can also choose easy and cheap, and let their emotions sit in the driver's seat. When the choices we make for children offer them real food for thought and a big world with natural consequences, we invite them to deal with reality in relationships that are trustworthy because they are true instead of easy.

New criteria for curriculum

Default education celebrates standardized achievement by young slaves—in bondage to the day to day demands of performing. Children work to earn, and to avoid punishment and shame. Tomorrow brings another day—of earning.

The best I can be is "better than you."

I wish this book could provide background music while you're reading this page. Imagine the opening scene of a Broadway blockbuster that examines the relationship between law and grace. Feel the heavy beating of the drums—in the orchestra and in your own heart.

The drums are the law in all the ways that remind an ex-convict of his past. The law gives him a number—instead of a name.

And even in this beginning scene, there is great hope. The song continues ... in freedom! It is a new day. For children and for all of us, mistakes are lessons to be learned under grace.

By design, curriculum selections offer children:

- The good, true, and beautiful things of life that we don't want them to miss.
- The power of inspiration.
- Everything life-giving, and nothing life-threatening.
- A ring, a robe, and a party (Luke 15:22, NIV)—especially when they struggle.

By design, school days offer children all the extravagant experiences we don't want them to miss. The capacity of time is an immovable boundary. We don't get more time because we waste it. In that regard, we fill childhood with the best books by the best authors. Heroes become our friends. Literature and poetry offer friendships. We meet and share life with people just like us—and not at all. Our world gets bigger with friends from far and wide.

Nature offers us fresh air—and we say, "Yes!" Together we linger in green grass, staring at clouds long enough for them to turn into stars. We experience science like an engineer—dissecting and designing in the ways that honor the systems that support life in us and on our planet. Math orders our steps. Music settles our souls and arouses our passions. Art invites us to risk new ways of expression. Leisure becomes our healing place—in all the ways that pausing to consider stabilizes our soul.

More than simply facts, data, and technique, children need inspiration. Childhood requires a life of the mind. I have spent hundreds of hours reading the work of Charlotte Mason, and am summarizing her ideas when I say, "A morning spent without encountering an idea is a morning wasted."

Our minds feed on ideas like our bodies feast on food. Like calories, inspiration is a force that invites us to move and contribute. Consider these ideas: bravery, freedom, mercy, and hope. When children allow themselves to be caught up by invisible forces for good, they have experienced the influence of love.

By design, education requires great care and protection. We can offer children things that are life-giving, and protect them against all things life-threatening. **We are keenly aware of the danger of guns in school. We are less keenly aware of the experiences that have the potential to turn children into shooters.** Hoop jumping, busy work, questions to answer at the end of the chapter to earn a grade ... a routine of meaninglessness puts a weight on our children's hearts.

Fear of asking for help or of being shunned in the places we're supposed to be loved—these experiences are life-threatening in the ways they demand their daily toll. Anxiety and depression stand at the door where love wants to be. In choosing curriculum, we must take care not to offer childhood on a toll road.

Children don't always trust the love that compels maturity. Consider the prodigal son. Children fight our help. They demand what they think they can never earn. When the prodigal son returned home, he was prepared to be a slave. The father welcomed him as a son—and gave him the gifts that reminded him he was a son, not a rebel.

The curriculum we offer, aiming at the target of maturity—even and especially to prodigals—is most like a ring and a robe and a party. Reminding our children of who God says they are offers them the strength to trust their true identity. Behavior is indeed the echo of belief.

Every book and assignment we choose can offer each child a true identity. Children learn who they are in relation to those they trust—and what we give them. The choices we make are not a reflection of their current earnings, what they can handle on their own, or what they deserve. The choices we make give our children a clearer reflection of who we see them to be, and who they are growing to be. A royal life thrives on nothing less.

Real considerations about making this change

What if you're ready to give these ideas an honest try? What if education by design is keeping you awake at night—not because it scares you, but instead, because you find yourself inspired?

On the first page of this book—in the very first paragraph—I said, "I've been waiting for you." Now that you've stayed with me all the way to chapter ten, I want to say, "Thank you. Thank you for risking this dream. It matters. There is great hope."

You may be happy to know you're not alone. Before I typed one word of this manuscript, a tribe was already gathering. We've wrestled and prayed. We've attended retreats. We've questioned. We still question.

And these questions are real:

- As a homeschool mom, can I keep doing the same things we've always done—and now intentionally do them with love?
- As a teacher—in a public, private or home school—do I need to throw out all of the curriculum I'm comfortable using and start over because we're choosing this new road?
- What if my children don't like the new curriculum? What if my children struggle?
- Is there a list for all the books I'll use each year, if I decide to lead my children on this new road?

- Do I have to use the books on the list, or can I choose books on my own?

Because we are building a new road, those of us who are risking this adventure can get queasy. We feel like Lewis & Clark, making a map instead of following one. We're not really comfortable doing things we're not yet good at, especially since we're in the habit of pleasing more than trusting. This adventure seems so foreign to the culture we've grown up in. We're comfortable knowing our place on the old road.

Can we just do school the way we've been doing it and believe this stuff about love in our hearts? **Can we put "love one another" on a sticker chart—or make it our screen saver, or the skill of the week—to remind ourselves about love while we're busy "being good?"**

Risking something this important requires a community of grace. Without friends trusting with us, we'll forget it's okay that everything's not okay. We'll forget that maturity doesn't look at all like perfection. We need others to remind us that we already have the DNA of a butterfly, even though at times all we can do is crawl on the ground—and today, we look very much like a caterpillar. Others need us to remind them, too.

These connections—in relationship with God, others, ideas, nature, and the real world—create the fuel we need to take this new adventure with our children. Like spontaneous combustion, the experiences we provide can produce the energy needed to travel through life, by design—more concerned about missing out than messing up.

The relationships we develop with Literature and Art and Math and Science and Nature will satisfy the desires of our spirit—and theirs. Satisfying physical hunger builds physical strength. Abiding in good and true and beautiful is a ticket to sail in a new world of thriving—that's very different than staying tied up in the harbor of surviving.

Experiences, not outcomes

By default, school requires children to please. Each subject is a taskmaster. Every day children must "be good," which invites them to hide when they are not good, or to look down on—or away from—others when they are good.

Transformational work is the kind that is difficult to grade. When we reduce assignments to a point system, the processing removes the nutrients. Instead of the teacher planning lessons based on getting enough grades to justify an average, education by design frees the teacher to offer rich experiences—and frees the students to respond beyond our power of measurement.

Brave love creates an atmosphere where it's safe to learn. Children don't have to be afraid of confusion. Children are offered rich experiences, not just assignments.

"I am the vine; you are the branches. Whoever abides in me and I in him, he it is that bears much fruit, for apart from me you can do nothing."

(John 15:5, ESV)

Chapter Eleven
We Can't Unsee

One year I taught world history to eighth graders. At least one day every week—starting in about October—I began class by drawing a long, horizontal line across the giant dry erase board that hung in the front of our classroom. Then I handed the dry erase marker to a student.

The students knew what to do. The first student chose an event, or period of time, or significant person in history—such as The Renaissance, or the birth of Jesus—and wrote this historical occurrence on the timeline on the board. They then handed the marker to another student. The next student added another historical occurrence—before or after the first one that had begun the exercise.

The students kept handing the marker to classmates until we had about 20-25 notes on our timeline. The "history review" was a good warm up. It provided our minds with a context from where we had come—and where we were heading—in our study of world history.

Are we listening to hope?
One spring day we decided to make some observations about our now extensive timeline. We looked for

patterns. One pattern we noticed—over time—was "war" and "peace." We found a cycle of war and peace, war and peace, until… the invention of the printing press.

After the printing press, there has been almost continual conflict. War. And we considered—what happened?

It took weeks of discussion, and much time in debate and wrestling in lunchtime conversations before the students landed on this theory:

Before "media" came on the scene, information, inspiration, and ideas were offered in person. Plays were performed on stage—not recorded and watched alone on Netflix. Literacy was low and books were valuable—so they were shared with care and interest and deep affection, often around a family table or at the feet of an elder.

Words and ideas exchanged in relationship offered life, and the meaning of life, from those who had lived through struggle. Relationships offered truth—as much as they had to give. And when life was a personal struggle for those who were young, and hope seemed lost leaning on their own understanding, the relationships that had offered truth about the past were strong and trustworthy.

Multi-generational communities offered strength—and hope—for the future. These relationships offered mature perspectives and shoulders to cry on—and love began to heal. When life is a struggle and wounds don't heal—anger erupts—and the war and peace cycle is stuck… in war.

Like now. Today, words can be cheap and the source of cheap words is not a trusted source. News is not often shared with care and interest and deep affection. News is more often offered with a motive of manipulation—instead of a motive of service.

Family mealtime is often discarded in favor of extra-curricular opportunities for the children—to perform. Conversations are rare—about the causes of war and peace—at home.

And we have a choice. We can choose to put rela-tionships first. We can offer words of comfort to our children. We can give them the love of wise words. We can listen to those who care and value—and hold us too important and precious to manipulate or use.

We can choose to listen together—as a family, and in trusted community. We can cry together. Pray together. Love and be loved. Love heals—not time. And peace comes.

We can choose to live in the cycle of war and peace again, instead of getting stuck in war. We can choose this for our families—and our schools.

By design, our children can grow up—in hope. Their children can, too.

Knowledge isn't enough.

The entirety of our life as a person is about learning to receive love. This is the life of a child. It is the original good news.

Twenty-first century schools don't yet offer our chil-dren love to drink when they are thirsty. Children are offered rules and knowledge instead. Our children are dehydrated. We're dehydrated. Like separating hydrogen from oxygen, our thirst is not quenched by the parts without the whole. Knowledge isn't enough.

In school, when children experience struggle—we find a label that explains why. "Why can't he learn?" "Why doesn't she know?" "Why do I have to tell them so many times?" Western civilization is characterized by rationalizing. We solve problems by explaining, or justifying, with logical reasons, even if these reasons are not true or appropriate.

In pursuit of more reason, we're not finding relief. The load we're carrying is heavier—burdened now by fresh justifications and recently developed labels. We're carrying our same problems, now with added pressure on our joints.

Our hoarding of "knowing" is taking its toll. Knowledge isn't holding us up. Instead of lightening our load, we're increasing our pain. And our pain is attracting more shame. Shame doesn't get fixed. Fear doesn't get fixed either.

But shame and fear can get resolved—in love.

If the chemical signature for water is H_2O, the signature for truth is L_2K. **Truth is two parts love for every one part of knowledge.**

The question we often ask is, "Will we know what to do?" A better question is, "Will we do what we know?"

Love helps us learn—and live in the truth.

Destiny, not just potential

Living up to his potential, Moses would've kept tending sheep—afraid of his failures, and hiding his shame. The burning bush was a risk. Trusting God, his destiny changed the course of a nation. All the people in Hebrews, chapter 11 are commended for their faith, not their perfect lives. Not their potential. They are commended for what God did *with* them, not how hard they worked *for* Him.

Trusting, there is great hope. Our destiny is not limited to our potential. Potential is the highest number of squares we can color in the graph paper life. Every square is a transaction. It's the best we can do. Destiny is the masterpiece God paints on the blank canvas—and we cannot make too much of God and what He has planned to do with us as we trust Him.

Trusting God, it is safe to fail—so it is safe to learn. Safe to learn is safe to risk. Safe to risk is safe to dream. Dreaming is deeply satisfying—because destiny never happens alone.

"And who knows but that you have come to your royal position for such a time as this?" Esther 4:14b, NIV.

Love will lead us.

Love will lead us, or we will not fully experience new life—or a dramatically changed experience in education. Whatever—or whoever—we trust to lead us through life will determine our experience. If we choose a program, we will go as far as the categories and levels allow—always aware of our place in an invisible hierarchy based on performing and acquiring.

If we choose to be led by the law's standards, we will be limited to the capacity of the law. We'll live hiding from the judgment, punishment, and condemnation waiting on every horizon—wishing we could choose adventure, and knowing failure is too big of a risk.

If we are led by a person, even ourselves—instead of a vision born from this new worldview—we will be swayed by chance desires, personal preferences, or whoever is going to get upset or be offended.

If we choose to be led by love, we will be limited only by the capacity of love.

God is our leader, by design. God gives us what we need, so we can live in the freedom and adventure He created us to enjoy. He doesn't require us to earn His gifts of love. He waits for our trust. Living loved, we grow up. We heal. We help. We contribute. We delight in living our dreams—and even risk living our destiny.

"No eye has seen, no ear has heard, and no mind has imagined, what God has prepared for those who love him," I Corinthians 2:9, NLT.

Chapter Twelve
Life by Design

Changing the way we offer education is changing the way we live life. When shame is attached to struggle, we experience life burdened with an attachment disorder of the worst kind. Shame tells us to hide at the very moment we need to run for help.

Struggle is a step toward maturity when I get because I need and because I am loved. Without shame, **I am stronger**—and in relationships, I get help to do what I could not do on my own. Now **I can**—because love is a process of meeting needs.

Life, as a student, is not just about "me." New life invites me to turn and trust the relationships with people who are helping me learn, and who are offering me opportunities to grow up. I am becoming trustworthy. Others are finding me a dependable source of help and care. This is living.

The weak become the strong … who help the weak become the strong.

What if it doesn't work?
That's the same question the Judaizers asked Paul in the New Testament. No, that's not exactly true. They

didn't ask Paul, "What if it doesn't work?" They insisted, "This isn't going to work, Paul!"

"You can't tell people Jesus really meant 'It is finished,'" they said. "You can't tell people they have great hope even when they struggle. They'll stop trying to be good. They're going to do Christianity-lite. They're going to sin on purpose—all because of grace. We'll all be a mess!"

That's my paraphrase of Romans, chapters 5-8.

And Paul's reply is my own response when people tell me that trusting love in education is coddling—or when they say, "It's not going to work, Janet!"

People may stop trying. Many already have. Some of them are children. In many ways, we're already a mess.

As believers, trusting who God says we are gives us a new identity. With a new heart, **we are fully equipped to love.** And we have the Holy Spirit continually living in us. We have been made new, so **we don't want to take advantage of God.** We are His children.

Some believers don't know this truth. They only know the stuff of religion—and the stuff of education by default. If more people stop trying, my hope is that they'll start trusting—more than themselves, and the hope of getting enough things right to find real joy.

Love is always right, but right is not always love.

And people can take advantage of law or grace. The freedom to choose is one of the greatest gifts of God. Together, we have enough strength to choose love.

Don't miss the beauty

I'm so delighted that one of my relationships of trust is with John Lynch and the people at Trueface. John's

"Two Roads" video on YouTube moved the compass needle in my soul away from the "pleasing God" road and pointed it due north—to the "trusting God" road. It has made all the difference.

John says friends don't stalk each other—they simply enjoy each other. That was in response to a comment I made on one of his posts on Facebook. For the past several years, I have read every word he has written in relationship with friends. Love speaks a new language—and I am hungry to speak it, too. John is my favorite language teacher.

He generously granted me permission to conclude this book with these words of love—a treasure he offered as a ransomed slave on social media. Because of Jesus, John is free. Because of Jesus, I am free. Thank you, John, for helping me trust what freedom really means.

Henri Nouwen writes these profound words in "Letters to Marc About Jesus."

"A lot of people have to expend so much energy on overcoming their low opinion of themselves that they seldom get round to asking about the purpose of their existence. And if they do, it is often out of fear."

He is, of course, correct. Learning who we are in Christ is not only to help us no longer drape ourselves in shame. It is of course that. Beautifully that. But the end game of apprehending grace and identity is for the privilege of entering into what we were put on earth to live out. We may call it destiny or simply living well. But ultimately our pleasure, joy and delight cannot come by seeking after them. They are a by-product of allowing this beautiful expression of Christ in us to be played out.

Reading this quote, I realized anew why we are so compelled to promote these truths of identity in Christ. Our vision must be to help others discover what they are freed from, and also to help them discover the wonder they've been freed into!

His quote gives even more urgency for me personally to live out of my identity in Christ. To ask the questions that get to form when I am no longer fighting to prove that I am enough, or hiding from the things I fear will confirm I am not enough.

When that game diminishes, such beautiful questions emerge.

"God, who do I get to love?"
"God, who has been waiting to love me well?"
"God, how can I receive your love, wildly and endlessly?"
"God, how do I best get to love those who don't know you?"
"God, what dreams and destiny are you forming in my heart?"
"God, who could I stand together with in a vision from You?"
"God, who can help me to mature into my destiny?"
"God, who can I help to mature into their destiny?"
"God, what brings my heart great joy?"
"God, what do we do best together?"
"God, thank you."

I don't want to miss the beauty of what He has for me to live out.

I missed the pleasure of that for far too long." ~ *John Lynch*

What Do We Do Now?

If you've read this far in this book, you may be ready to trust something new. Life by design, not default, is a gift buried deep in our DNA. Deep calls to deep. We are created to respond.

Life by design is a wild ride. We are all pioneers. Settling only happens to pioneers when we're in need of comfort or rest—or when someone else does. Settling of this kind is "settled" by design—not default. Comfort doesn't stop at pain relief. It goes all the way to healing. Resting is more than relaxation. Restoration happens. Healing and restoration are designed for pioneers, not settlers.

God only knows how many ways you could take a step in the direction of freedom—not away from struggle or truth, but away from fear and shame. This list simply gets your mind going in the direction of design, not default:

- **Make your home a safe place to grow up.** Disconnect struggle from shame—not truth. Declare your home an "adolescence-free" zone and help your children grow up to be young adults—by design.
- **Intentionally seek out and connect in trusting relationships, and find a community of grace for yourself.** If you can't find one, build one. Be loved, and love one another. By design, we need each other. The only thing God said was "not good" was for man to be alone.
- **Choose healthy vulnerability—for your sake and for your family.** Find help resolving your

own issues. As my friends say who wrote *The Cure & Parents*, "When your children are young, being the parent carries enough control to handle them. But if you don't grow up as they grow older, your immaturity will stunt their maturity at the level of your own. And no measure of control can handle that."[12]

- **Commit to a work-leisure-play-rest cycle, instead of perform-pain relief cycle, in your life.** Help your children enjoy this life, too—by design, not default.

- **Mentor children and young adults in learning how to enjoy handwork and leisure skills.** There are plenty of programs out there already that offer jump houses, slime races, and dance parties. Be someone who helps kids learn to garden, knit, build a fort, restore a lawnmower, cross-stitch, bake bread, or sew a quilt. Take a young person to a museum or a symphony. Help children by offering relationships that settle their souls.

- **Become a High Trust Leader.** Trueface.org offers a 16-week High Trust Leader Course (HTLC) that explores the truth about who God says He is, and who He says you are. You will be instructed, challenged, and encouraged in how to develop High Trust Communities. The HTLC provides teams of any size the ability to dive deeper into the gospel of God's grace which will deepen your influence. This course can shift your *worldview*, not simply fine-tune your current world. This

---

12 *The Cure and Parents*, Bill & Grace Thrall, John & Stacey Lynch, Bruce & Janet McNicol, CrossSection, 2016.

course can expand and deepen your *influence*, not simply offer leadership skills.

- **Host a Grace Changes Everything retreat.** The retreats are a simple way to explore grace with your community. Hosted by people like you, these retreats consist of video stories, facilitator-guided discussions, reading for reflection and thought-provoking questions, spread over just one evening and the next morning. If you want to step further into exploring grace with those around you, hosting this retreat is a great starting point. Visit my website <u>janetnewberry.com</u> or <u>trueface.org</u> to learn more.

- **Host a John 15 Academy retreat.** Janet Newberry Educational Consulting, LLC offers retreats that invite you to experience the difference of a new approach in education. The retreats are designed for homeschool families, and for leaders and pioneers in education. We'd love to share this hope with people offering education to young people who are incarcerated, children who are in orphanages, and anyone ready to risk a new worldview. An ideal retreat includes a group of 8-14, beginning on a Friday evening and concluding on Sunday afternoon. The retreat offers each participant an opportunity to experience the difference of transformational–instead of transactional–education. Time is scheduled for you to ask questions and get practical answers for you, your family, or your organization.

- **Join us in our dream to share this message of hope.** We'd love to hear your ideas and have a

conversation about dreaming together. Send me
an email at janet@john15academy.com.

"My response is to get down on my knees before the Father,
this magnificent Father
who parcels out all heaven and earth. I ask him to
strengthen you by his Spirit—
not a brute strength but a glorious inner strength—that
Christ will live in you
as you open the door and invite him in.
And I ask him that with both feet planted firmly on love,
you'll be able to take in with all followers of Jesus
the extravagant dimensions of Christ's love.
Reach out and experience the breadth!
Test its length! Plumb the depths! Rise to the heights!
Live full lives, full in the fullness of God."
(Ephesians 3: 14-19, The Message)

Appendix A
The John 15
Academy
Community

Many of the pioneers currently risking this new road in education are offering a John 15 Academy education to their children. John 15 Academy is an educational entity—and our 501(c)3.

Membership in the John 15 Academy online community offers support for homeschool families and other educational pioneers that is unique in two key ways:

- The benefits of a John 15 Academy Premium Membership are specifically designed for parents who want to build and protect healthy relationships with their children. Being both a parent and a teacher is difficult; relationships can get strained. When relationships get strained, homeschool can become a nightmare. We believe if we encourage and support you, you will be better equipped to encourage and support your children. If you want to better help your children, membership in this online community is created just for you.

- A John 15 Academy education is different. Unlike other educational programs that aim at test scores and performance standards, a John 15 Academy education aims first at supporting maturity in our children by building relationships of trust at home. My research shows that when we aim at performance, relationships and maturity always suffer—and when we aim at relationships and maturity, performance goes off the charts.

We want to help you, so you can help your children. Visit the "At School" page on our website to learn more about the specific benefits of joining this online community. https://janetnewberry.com/at-school/

John 15 Academy Welcome Home Appendix B Education by Design—Five Schools

Three intentional traditions on this new road in education at John 15 Academy are:

- student groupings,
- School schedules,
- and a broad and rigorous curriculum.

Instead of age-based grade levels, this new road designates five "Schools" for students, based on academic needs, and relational maturity:

Primary School (students attend for 1-2 years)
Elementary School for Young Children (students attend for 1-2 years)

Elementary School for Older Children (students attend for 3-4 years)
Intermediate School (students attend for 3-4 years)
High School (students attend for 4-5 years)

The **Primary School -**
serves children who are 5 or 6 years old.
The School offers approximately 9-12 hours of instruction. The suggested schedule is Monday, Wednesday, and Friday mornings—approximately 3-4 hours each day. The remainder of the week is for play and leisure and rest, and the practical work of the home. This "new life-cycle" is a part of the schedule for all five Schools.

Children in Primary School learn that God's design for our lives is connection in healthy relationships. Children respond to the initiative of parents and teachers who consistently offer to connect—and reconnect—in relationships of trust. Young children learn that "joy" is our normal state. Joy means "it's good to be me here with you." In relationships with adults who encourage them to fully experience a full and free life—and all the feelings that come with this life—children learn to "return to joy"[13] from every unpleasant emotion—and not to get stuck in destructive emotions. This one skill is the foundation for a lifetime of emotional health.

Children learn to receive "yes" and "no" and "not yet" as words of love, trusting the direction and protection of a love that knows them better than they know themselves. Children learn to celebrate with, and lend

---

13 *Living From The Heart Jesus Gave You*, James G. Friesen, E. James Wilder, Anne M. Bierling, Rick Koepcke, & Maribeth Poole, Shepherd's House, 2013.

strength to their friends, and remind them of who God says they are, too.

Children in The Primary School will begin a relationship with these subjects and experiences:
Literature / Read Aloud / Poetry
Reading Instruction
Phonics Instruction
Handwriting
Number Sense / Arithmetic
Gardening/Nature Study
Art/Picture Study
Handwork
Bible
Memorization / Recitation
Geography
Illustrating Thank You Notes
Music / Composer Study
Play
Practical Life
Cooking
Puppets / Puppet Shows
Rest

Elementary School for Young Children -
serves children who are 6 or 7 years old.

The School offers approximately 15-20 hours of instruction each week. The suggested schedule is Monday - Friday mornings, approximately 3-4 hours each day.

Students in the Elementary School for Young Children learn to take responsibility for caring for themselves in the ways of practical life. Young children learn to read and write and measure and calculate. They learn to organize and restore order to chaos. Table manners and polite and inclusive table conversations add value to the experience of meals for everyone. Laundry, yard work, and simple home maintenance jobs are a few of the ways young children can begin to experience significance in the story of their family. Maturity always invites us to see the world as bigger than ourselves.

Language development is vital in the Elementary School for Young Children, as it is in all stages of maturity, in the ways that language helps us articulate our needs and talk truthfully about our emotions. Intentional curriculum selections help support this development. Asking for help is an important habit for children learning to take care of themselves, as is the habit of humility.

Talking truthfully about emotions is an important component of metabolizing the experience of fear-based emotions, and helps prevent these emotions from finding a place to take root in our children's souls.

Children in this School will continue growing in the same subjects they were introduced to in The Primary School. As children mature, their attention spans mature, too. They enjoy longer stories; they are capable of attending in longer conversations. As maturity builds, instruction supports continued academic growth. New subjects introduced in this School are:

Transcription, and

Becoming a Writer - Dictated Narration

The **Elementary School for Older Children** -
serves children who are 7-10 years old.

The School offers approximately 25-30 hours of instruction each week. The suggested schedule is Monday - Friday, approximately 5-6 hours each day.

Students in the Elementary School for Older Children are building personal capacity, and are developing enough perseverance to do hard things. Children are learning to experience a full range of emotions, without letting their emotions hijack their behavior. They are beginning to build a life of integrity, understanding that choices are made based on personal values and convictions, rather than chance desires or personal preferences.

Instead of focusing on "being good," children are beginning to notice the impact and influence of their behavior on others. Because they desire their impact and influence to be love, they delight in discovering that loving others is the true path to experiencing goodness.

Students in the Elementary School for Older Children are growing in relationship with these subjects and experiences: (New subjects introduced in this School are in bold.)

Literature / Read Aloud / Poetry

Reading Instruction and Phonics Instruction (only as needed)

Handwriting (cursive - when appropriate)

Arithmetic

Grammar

Science

History

Keyboarding (as needed & as appropriate)
**Becoming a Writer - Written Narration and writing
    paragraphs (as appropriate)**
Gardening / Nature Study
Art / Picture Study
Handwork
Bible
Memorization / Recitation
Geography
Thank You Notes
Music / Composer Study
Play
Practical Life
Cooking

The Intermediate School

serves children, who are becoming young adults,
ages 11-14.

The Intermediate School schedule includes approximately 30-35 hours of both formal instruction and autonomous work* each week. The suggested schedule is Monday - Friday, approximately 6-7 hours each day.

*Autonomous work is different than independent work. The goal of education on a new road is not independence, but rather dependence—on the new life of Christ in me and the indwelling power of the Holy Spirit.

Autonomous implies having self-governance. As new creations, young adults can trust their new heart. Autonomous work is done in a mature relationship with myself, and from an internal motivation. In contrast, the history of independent school work has sometimes been from the motive of earning a good grade, or the motive of compliance—rather than the motive of trusting obedience.

Students in Intermediate School are becoming young adults, who are experiencing mutually satisfying relationships. As young adults, students are beginning to care for others—as they have learned to care for themselves. Instead of living from the motive of pleasing others—or manipulating others to get what they want, young adults are learning to enjoy relationships of trust with their peers, younger children, and trustworthy mentors. These relationships offer strength, and young adults are now building the capacity they need to remain stable, even in difficult times.

Spiritual Maturity is added to the curriculum in Intermediate School and continues in High School. Students will read books selected to deepen their theological understanding of their faith, and explore important topics in the life of a believer—such as forgiveness, grace, repentance, trust, shame, love …

Students in Intermediate School are growing in relationship with these subjects and experiences: (New subjects introduced in this School are in bold.)

Literature / Read Aloud / Poetry
Mathematics
Spiritual Maturity
Science
History
Keyboarding
Grammar (as needed)
Becoming a Writer - Written Narration, paragraphs, and essays

Gardening / Nature Study
Art / Picture Study
Handwork
Bible
Memorization / Recitation
Geography
Thank You Notes
Music / Composer Study
Physical Conditioning / Sports
Practical Life

The High School
serves young adults, ages 14 and older.

The High School schedule includes 32-40+ hours of both formal instruction and autonomous work each week.

Students in High School are mature young adults, growing in their experiences of contributing to the community—including their home and family. Young adults know how to return to joy—and can help others return to joy, too. The primary focus of relational maturity as a young adult is learning to take care of two people simultaneously (self and one other).

Helping younger students with their school work, caring for younger siblings, cooking for the family, babysitting, serving as an assistant coach or mother's helper, and/or helping to care for an aging relative are vital experiences that support ongoing maturity during High School.

Students in High School are maturing in their relationships with these subjects and experiences:

Literature / Poetry
Mathematics
Spiritual Maturity
Science
History
Keyboarding (as needed)
Becoming a Writer - Written Narration, paragraphs, and essays
Gardening / Nature Study*
Art / Picture Study*
Handwork*
Bible
Thank You Notes*
Music / Composer Study*
Physical Conditioning / Sports
Practical Life (including vocational training as appropriate)

*In High School, subjects such as Picture Study, Nature Study, Handwork, and Composer Study can provide a respite—and a gift of leisure—in each student's educational journey. Relationships such as these are offered to add beauty and passion and balance to an otherwise demanding daily schedule.

*Time spent writing thank you notes provides an opportunity of rest and healing for the brain. The brain cannot be anxious and thankful at the same time. Thank You Notes are not to be required as an act of compliance, but rather experienced as a time of refreshment.

Appendix C
A New Worldview

After the cross and resurrection of Jesus Christ, our purpose is no longer to strive to earn an identity—or the approval and acceptance that may come with success. Our purpose is to keep trusting the God who loved us enough to offer us the identity of His Son—Christ-in-me, and Christ-in-you.

A new heart is ours for the trusting. We have a shame-free identity, too—even when we struggle. Trusting this Christ-in-me identity, I can live a life of hope instead of fear. Because we trust and experience the love and forgiveness of God, we find the freedom we could never earn under the law. We are free to love, instead of simply perform.

Law cannot restore the world; law only has the power to condemn. Trusting the law, we live measuring outcomes according to law's standards. Law bears the fruit of judgment and punishment; ask any child who's spent more than a day or two at school.

Trusting Christ, we live new lives, trusting His life, now observable in us. Love knows that what is inside us will come out. "The fruit of the Spirit is love, joy, peace, patience, kindness, goodness, faithfulness, gentleness, and self-control. Against such things, there is no law," Galatians 5:22-23, KJV.

A Worldview Changed by Grace

- We believe God is who He says He is; God is love (I John 4:8). God is always the initiator in relationship: He always moves towards us in love and truth. God's love is fully committed; we never have to earn His love. His is the love of a servant—attentive to our needs. His love is faithful; completely trustworthy. God's corrective love leads us and provides direction; His "jealous for us" love sets boundaries and provides protection. God's affirmations tell us our significance—in His heart and in our world.

- We believe the original good news changed everything—and offers, not a better way of doing the old life, but a new way and a new life.

- We believe we access this new life trusting God; we believe we grow up in this new life by trusting God. Trust is the door that opens to God's love—and the love of others.

- We believe the moment we trust God, we are given the gift of a new nature—and the indwelling power of the Holy Spirit. I am no longer a sinner, striving to become a saint; I am a now a saint who sometimes sins. This new nature is Christ-in-me and Christ-in-you; 100% righteous because of His life abiding in us. Christ-in-me and the reality of the Holy Spirit abiding in me equips me to live my new life with strength greater than my own. Love, joy, peace, patience, kindness, goodness, faithfulness, gentleness, and self-control are mine for the trusting. I did not have this power in my old nature.

- We believe sin is a force—whose motive is to work against God's perfect design. Sin damages and kills. This damage and death is the punishment of sin—not God.

- We believe shame is a force—whose motive is to convince us to hide from God and from each other, especially when we need help. Shame comes in the shadow of sin. Shame offers us an invalid identity; shame names us by our struggle.

- We believe grace is Jesus. His blood paid for our sins once and for all. He always expresses Himself in unconditional, transformational love. Grace matures us as we continue to trust God and experience His love. We believe grace is the stuff of miracles. "He who is in you is greater than he (Satan) who is in the world [of sinful mankind]," I John 4:4, AMP.

- We believe our behavior is the mirror of our beliefs. When I trust who God says He is, I trust His love for me—and I experience His love that changes my behavior. I let Him meet my real needs. When I trust who God says I am, I trust His righteousness in me; I trust the fruit of the Spirit in me to give me encouragement and strength to live a life of love. When I trust who God says you are, I see your needs and love you in the ways God designed for me to love you. I remind you often of your true identity, and let you remind me of mine. I let you see my real needs, too—and receive your love in the ways God designed you to love me.

- We believe the motive of this new life is "be loved" and "love one another." This motive is very different than "fix my sin" or "get everything right." When my motive is "fix my sin," I am trying to do what only the cross of Christ can do. When my motive is "love one another," I am trusting the power of my new nature. In my maturity, I discover I am sinning less and getting more things right.
- We believe love is a process of meeting needs. When our needs are met, the weak become strong. We believe our God-given needs include: commitment, unearned love, servant love, faithful love, corrective love, "jealous for"/protective love, and affirmation. God completely meets our needs— and He often uses others to meet them, too.
- We believe maturity is the fruit of our trust—just as salvation is the gift of our trust. As I trust the truth about who God is, and who He says I am—I grow up. As my maturity grows, so will my character and my capacities.
- We believe—in all the truth of our new nature— that joy is our normal state. Our definition for "joy" is "it's good to be me here with you." We build joy strength as we trust, bond, and live life in healthy relationships. Experiencing the grace gifts of forgiveness and repentance, we learn to return to joy from every unpleasant emotion. We believe in owning the influence and impact of our sin in the lives of others; forgiveness can

rebuild trust—so we can experience each other's love again.

- We believe "in this world we will have struggle" and personal humility offers opportunities to receive help when we trust God and others. "The goal of the Christian life is not in what you can produce, but how you learn to depend upon Christ in what you cannot produce" (John Lynch).

- We believe in life lived in relationships of trust and communities of grace; we believe these communities speak the language of love and truth. We believe these relationships offer protection from shame, blame, condemnation, manipulation, and unmet needs. We give others permission to protect us in these healthy ways.

- We believe trusting our new commandment, "Love one another," equips us to be grace carriers that others can trust. We don't count mistakes; counting tempts us to commit other sins. We take our sin and mistakes seriously, not because they disqualify us or speak in any way about our identity, but because sin and mistakes hurt us and hurt others. Hurt invites shame and lies and separation. The cross of Christ erased the sin from my report card and gave me a shame-free identity. Grace can restore our relationships with others, too.

- We believe in abiding in a big and beautiful world—trusting the love of God as He offers us beauty, good work, inspiration, challenge, delight, grand affections, leisure, and rest.

Acknowledge-
ments

"There is nothing in life comparable to being grateful;
I can't be grateful without being in need. But far more
than the humility is to acknowledge that I am needy."
~ from The Allender Center

I am grateful beyond words to my husband. Doug Newberry—you love me well. The last words I hear before I fall asleep every night are "I love you, Janet. Thank you for being my friend." The first words I hear every morning are, "Good morning, beautiful."

In between good morning and good night, you lead me in a wild and crazy trusting God adventure. You listen. No matter how long it takes—you hear my heart. You cook and wash dishes and empty the black tank in Freedom, our Airstream. Laundry isn't something I've done since we started putting quarters in the machines in RV park laundromats. You are a servant.

You are a first responder to my God-given needs— and you never keep score. You give and serve and love and laugh and forgive me and ask me for forgiveness because it is who you are, not because you're trying to get something from me. I am never in debt to you because of your love and care—I am always richer and exceedingly blessed. Your love transforms me—for good.

Thank you for teaching me, "Don't walk naked in front of the bullies." You remind me that choosing vulnerability in safe relationships is key. When I admitted to you that writing a book about changing education feels like walking naked in front of some bullies, you quickly reminded me, "You never walk alone." Thank you for protecting me, Doug.

I will always treasure the memories of the night you read this book aloud to me—from start to finish. My "final edits" were due and I wanted to hear the whole thing—as a way of settling my soul, convinced that the words on the page offered the real hope of brave love. You started reading aloud chapter one at 6:00 p.m. on a Sunday night, and finished reading Appendix C at 2:00 a.m. the next Monday morning. We laughed and cried many times in those eight hours. I need you, and I am grateful. I could never write a book about Brave Love without you.

I am grateful to my friends at Trueface. There are too many of you to list here: authors, Board members, faculty members, staff… Thank you for all you offer in our world that is the grace that changes everything. Without Trueface, I'd still be spending too much of my life trying to please and earn instead of taste and see. The Lord is good! New life really is lived from a place of freedom instead of bondage. Who knew? God knew. And He knew I'd find you and your Two Roads analogy. I need you, and I am grateful.

I am grateful to my agent, Cynthia Ruchti, and to Janet Grant, President at Books and Such Literary

Management. God knew. He knew we'd find each other, Cynthia, and you would talk me out of my "I don't want to write a book" denial. I'll always be thankful for the day you called to invite me to be your client. You shared a conversation you'd had with Janet Grant. You told her my story and asked, "What do I do with 'my Janet?'" Her response was, "What if God is giving you a gift? What are you going to do with it?"

Thank you for calling me a gift, Janet. Thank you for treating me like a gift, Cynthia. Thank you for believing that I have something to offer the world in books. Because you believe it, I believe it, too. Your love continues to separate struggle from shame in the life of this rookie Bookie. I need you, and I am grateful.

Together, there is great hope.

66326993R00085

Made in the USA
Columbia, SC
17 July 2019